I began ministry as a teenager, preaching to inmates in prisons in South Carolina. Three decades later, I find myself as a pastor helping people daily overcome trauma, addiction, and shame. Also, my own family members have wrestled with the pattern of addiction, recovery, relapse, and repeat. I know firsthand how important this book is for the church, our culture, and every individual who's ever messed up and wants to start over (but wonders where to begin). God offers us grace to start over, and the mistakes we've made actually benefit us by making us wiser, stronger, and more resilient. Chris has laid out a simple, biblical, doable approach to embracing our mess as the pathway to God's miracle of new beginnings.

CLAYTON KING
Pastor, evangelist, and author of 18 books, including *Reborn*, *Stronger*, and *Overcome*

Perfect people won't need this book . . . but the rest of us are deeply thankful that our God gives second chances! Chris Rappazini has a heart for people and a passion for teaching God's Word. If you are struggling to find the next step forward or trying to understand how God is at work in your story, this book is for you.

JAMIE JANOSZ
Managing Editor, *Today in the Word*, Moody Bible Institute

Biblical, practical, insightful, and wonderfully written! *Moving Forward After Messing Up* will stir your emotions, inspire your heart, and restore your hope. Moreover, you will be motivated by a holy compulsion to comfort, encourage, and strengthen those who need Christ's forgiveness and restoration.

KEITH R. KRELL
Senior Pastor, Crossroads Bible Church Bellevue, WA

Chris Rappazini offers a contemporary, fresh, readable, and applicable approach for those who messed up, which is every human on this planet at some time. His treatment is illustrated, biblical, merciful, and hopeful. The chapters themselves are just the length needed in this distracted time while sufficiently covering the subject. Chris strikes the right balance between Christian discipline and redemption. He does not excuse the biblical or contemporary characters, but he does offer the hope of a way out and up. You either know someone or know yourself well enough to hand this book to them—not with a patronizing hand from above but with a friendly touch from alongside.

JOEL C. GREGORY
Professor of Preaching, George W. Truett Endowed Chair of Preaching and Evangelism, Baylor's George W. Truett Theological Seminary

The God of the Bible is a God of grace, and He creates an ecosystem of grace and restoration while simultaneously being the essence of truth. We need this kind of restoration in our world today. In this book, Dr. Rappazini shows us how we might cultivate it.

BRAD COOPER
Lead Pastor of Culture & Direction, NewSpring Church

Some of us can hide our painful mistakes. Others must grapple with the shame of failures laid bare for the world to see. Whatever your circumstance, Chris Rappazini invites you to walk with Him toward a hopeful future. *Moving Forward After Messing Up* is a deeply personal, accessible, and practical guide for those seeking a way out of brokenness.

BRIAN DAHLEN
Host, *Mornings with Brian* on WCRF, Moody Radio Cleveland; creator and host of *The Grandfather Effect* podcast

MOVING
FORWARD
AFTER
MESSING
UP

A New Future
with the God
of Second
Chances

DR. CHRIS RAPPAZINI

MOODY PUBLISHERS
CHICAGO

© 2024 by
CHRIS RAPPAZINI

Scriptures taken from the Holy Bible, New International Version®, NIV®. Copyright ©1973, 1978, 1984, 2011 by Biblica, Inc.™ Used by permission of Zondervan. All rights reserved worldwide. www.zondervan.com The "NIV" and "New International Version" are trademarks registered in the United States Patent and Trademark Office by Biblica, Inc.™

Some content has been adapted from articles by the author published in Today in the Word.

All emphasis in Scripture has been added.

Edited by Pamela J. Pugh
Interior design: Puckett Smartt
Cover design: Kaylee Dunn
Cover background of color smoke copyright © 2023 by Corona Borealis/Adobe Stock (270972208). All rights reserved. Cover element of ink splat copyright © 2024 by zzorik/Adobe Stock (371939157). All rights reserved.

Library of Congress Cataloging-in-Publication Data

Names: Rappazini, Chris, author.
Title: Moving forward after messing up : a new future with the god of second chances / Dr. Chris Rappazini.
Description: Chicago, IL : Moody Publishers, 2024. | Includes bibliographical references. | Summary: "What happens when we honestly face our mess and seek God? Can beauty, love, or hope follow? Failure and regret can deepen our character. Those who seem permanently wrecked can experience joy, freedom, and a newfound dream. Rappazini takes us beyond despair to biblically based forgiveness and a faithful future"-- Provided by publisher.
Identifiers: LCCN 2023052840 | ISBN 9780802432827 (paperback) | ISBN 9780802471871 (ebook)
Subjects: LCSH: Failure (Psychology)--Religious aspects--Christianity. | Forgiveness, | Redemption. | BISAC: RELIGION / Christian Ministry / Discipleship | RELIGION / Christian Living / Personal Growth
Classification: LCC BT730.5 .R377 2024 | DDC 248.4--dc23/eng/20240206
LC record available at https://lccn.loc.gov/2023052840

Originally delivered by fleets of horse-drawn wagons, the affordable paperbacks from D. L. Moody's publishing house resourced the church and served everyday people. Now, after more than 125 years of publishing and ministry, Moody Publishers' mission remains the same—even if our delivery systems have changed a bit. For more information on other books (and resources) created from a biblical perspective, go to www.moodypublishers.com or write to:

Moody Publishers
820 N. LaSalle Boulevard
Chicago, IL 60610

1 3 5 7 9 10 8 6 4 2

Printed in the United States of America

*To all those courageous enough
to turn their setback into a comeback,
this book is dedicated to your inspiring journey.*

CONTENTS

HOW DID IT GET TO THIS?

How did it get to this?
Could it possibly get any worse?
What do I do now?
How long will this take?

Have these questions above ever crossed your mind?
Maybe you asked them after finalizing a divorce or being let go from your job. Perhaps you whispered them under your breath in an empty hospital room or an overcrowded jail cell. Maybe these questions came as you realized your overspending has caught up with you and your debt is overwhelming. Perhaps someone asked you similar questions in your church's small group or even during group time at a rehabilitation center. Or maybe, like me, it was after a phone call with a loved one who seemingly had just hit rock bottom. Well, if you never read another page of this book, at least walk away knowing this: you are not alone in asking these questions . . . although, at times, it can certainly feel that way.

Millions of people, just like you, have scratched their heads, wondering, "How did things spiral out of control?" Sometimes it happens gradually, like a slow-moving hurricane waiting to make landfall.

Other times, the storms of life come like a flash flood or deadly tornado with no warning, and you are left trying to keep your head above water or diving for shelter. Regardless of how you or your loved one got there, the reality is, you know something must change.

Easier said than done.

Everybody loves a redemption story. Whether it is in sports or on the movie screen, we crave people who get a second chance after they have fallen. But why does it always seem to work out for everyone else? It would be amazing if we could wake up one morning and our relationships with our parents or kids were restored. Or that addiction miraculously disappeared. Or the consequences of those poor decisions had magically vanished. Unfortunately, life is not written with sidewalk chalk, it is written with a permanent marker. But that doesn't mean the future has to look the same as the past and our mess can't turn into a powerful message.

Did you know that the Bible is essentially a book about people who fail? They failed in their relationships, marriages, careers, walk with God, and much more. But the Bible is also a book about moving forward after messing up. So, if you have ever felt like a failure or need a second chance, if you have neglected vital relationships, need to move on after a nasty divorce, start a new career path, get a handle on your finances, beat an addiction, overcome depression or anxiety, or—fill in the blank—then keep reading. Explore with me as we look at stories from Scripture as well as modern-day stories of those whose past helped them propel their future.

This isn't a book about sitting back and watching God do His thing—I want to assure you there is more to it than that. You have an active role to play. Whether you are going through a challenging season or watching and waiting for a loved one to snap out of it, there is action to be taken. I want to help you rethink what it means that

God gives multiple chances, what steps you should take, and what land mines to avoid.

MEET MY BROTHER

When I was pastoring, our church loved celebrating the success stories about people being healed of cancer or overcoming an addiction, testimonies of restored marriages, and prodigals coming home. But for every redemptive victory, there were scores of others that were a mixture of losses and grief. Walking alongside someone during their darkest days is heartbreaking. You see the hurt. You feel the pain. And those days turn into months and then into years. What makes it even harder is when that person is part of your own family.

When our ninety-four-year-old grandmother died, it was my responsibility to notify my older brother Nick of her passing. I don't know if it was my task because I was his brother, the so-called spiritual leader of the family, or if it was because I was the only one still on speaking terms with him. Although "speaking terms" is a stretch as I only had talked to him a handful of times over the past several years.

Nick was notorious for being difficult to reach. He was homeless and didn't always have a working cellphone. I tried reaching the one friend of his I knew, and she said that she hadn't talked to him in weeks. However, after several attempts over multiple days with no successful contact, my mind started to go to dark places of where he could be, what could have happened to him, or what he could have done to himself. I was actually relieved when Nick's friend sent me a screenshot of his name on the local police department's website of people who were recently arrested.

After calling the sheriff's department and informing the desk worker about the nature of my call, I was able to speak to Nick for fifteen minutes. There was so much I wanted to say in those fifteen minutes. So many questions to ask. But I found myself just trying to listen to him explain his side of the story. After our phone call was over, I ended up asking myself those questions:

How did it get to this?
Could it possibly get any worse?
What do I do now?
How long will this take?

Along with examining the nature of God, delving into second chances, and exploring the redemptive narratives in the Bible, throughout this book I want to share with you the story of how my family and I have been walking alongside my brother during his ups and downs and battles with alcohol, drugs, and mental health issues. But spoiler alert, Nick is not where he ultimately wants to be, even if he is in a much better place than where he was. We are still walking this journey with him, as I imagine you are still walking this journey yourself, or maybe alongside your brother, sister, child, grandchild, spouse, partner, or friend. This is not a book about how things worked out flawlessly for me and so I'm telling you how you can get there too. Instead, I want to travel the journey with you. Because this book is not about my brother and me. This book is ultimately about you, your loved ones, and God.

I know that life can be challenging, and it's easy to feel lost or disconnected. But even in those moments, God is at work in your life, with a perfect plan designed to bring you joy and fulfillment. You might feel that you've strayed too far from Him, or that you do not deserve His love. But the truth is, God's love is endless, and His mercy knows no bounds. No matter what you've done, you're never beyond His reach and healing touch.

GOD IS STANDING ON
THE SHORELINE OF YOUR LIFE

Fishermen are some of the hardest-working people I know. Growing up in a small fishing village in Florida, I got to know several. They were up before the sun, getting ready for the day and setting out to sea regardless of the weather. The funny thing is, they couldn't imagine doing anything else. Fishermen love to fish.

Several of Jesus' followers were fishermen, including Peter. He loved to fish. What is unthinkable is that when he put down his nets to follow Jesus, he also put aside his profession and his lifestyle (Matthew 4:18–22). But even after Jesus' death and resurrection, Peter still wasn't sure if he could live a life apart from fishing. For him, fishing was everything. It was what he would have thought about the moment he woke up and what was on his mind before he shut his eyes at night.

In John 21, we encounter Peter back out on the water, fishing. After his three denials of Christ (Mark 14:66–72), Peter likely felt he had placed himself outside of Jesus' inner circle and, therefore, retreated and went back to his old ways and his first love. That's right—even Jesus' best bud had to learn how to move forward after messing up.

Many times, like Peter, we start off on the right path, but then we find ourselves in a bind and revert to the life we once had. We turn back to our past and our former tendencies. We return to our first loves. God wants you to love Him more than anything else. When Peter went back to fishing, he certainly didn't expect for Jesus to keep pursuing him, let alone talk about those courtyard denials, but that is what Jesus did. Here's the thing—Jesus is pursuing you too, and He wants to talk about your past.

In John 21, Jesus showed up on the shore of Peter's life. "Cast your net on the other side of the boat," shouted a familiar voice from the beach. The miraculous catch that ensued immediately got Peter's attention. He realized whose voice it was, none other than his friend and Savior, Jesus (see John 21:6–7). Peter instantly plunged into the water and swam ashore. Similarly to when they first met, Jesus had surprised him with an unbelievable catch. But this time, it was different. Peter was in need of a second chance.

Jesus wasn't the only thing waiting for Peter on the shore. He had started a charcoal fire with fish on it nearby. What would have seemed like a friendly gesture to most would have reminded Peter of something completely different: his rejection of Christ in the courtyard not too many nights ago. You see, after Jesus was arrested in the Garden of Gethsemane, Peter was terrified that the authorities might capture and torture him too. So, while hiding in the shadows among the courtyards, attempting to observe what was happening behind the courthouse walls, Peter had warmed himself by the charcoal fires.

Jesus was giving Peter another chance. He was giving Peter a path to move forward after messing up.

However, people became curious about his presence and questioned him, "You aren't one of his disciples too, are you?" "Didn't I see you with him in the garden?" Peter emphatically denied any affiliation with Jesus. After his third denial, though, he heard a rooster crow off in the distance. The bird's call reminded him of Jesus' words spoken to him a few hours earlier, "This very night, before the rooster crows, you will disown me three times" (Matthew 26:34). Now on the beach, several days after Jesus' death and resurrection, Peter and Jesus have some unfinished business to attend to.

After their morning fish fry, Jesus takes Peter for a stroll down the beach and memory lane. Then, the Prince of Peace turns directly to Peter, and asks him three times, "Peter, do you love me?" (see John 21: 15–17). Peter quickly answered, "Of course! You know that I love You."

Let's be clear: Peter's declaration of loving the Lord three times did not erase his three denials just days before. However, it did create an avenue for a deeper relationship with Jesus. With each question, Jesus was giving Peter another chance. He was giving Peter a path to move forward after messing up. Peter, the fisherman, would finally retire, and permanently drop his nets, and Peter, the follower of Jesus, would never turn back again.

I want to take a moment to remind you of something truly extraordinary—God wants what is best for you, and He is doing something powerful in your life right now. No matter how many times you have turned away from Him, He never stops loving you. He is always standing on the shore of your life, calling you back to Himself. He may even want to use your past to change someone else's future.

LET'S GET STARTED

So why wait? I'm convinced that if you travel this journey with me, you will be one step closer to understanding yourself (or your loved one) and the God of Second Chances better. You will be able to view your past through a new set of lenses. You will be able to have a stronger relationship with God and those around you. And you might be able to find the peace and joy you've been desiring. But I can also guarantee it won't be easy. It will take self-reflection and action. Yes, it won't be easy, but it will be worth it.

My hope is that in these pages, you will see just how many do-overs God gives people. Perhaps even more importantly, why He gives so many opportunities instead of turning people away. You will learn how important humility and forgiveness are to moving forward. In addition, you will understand why we keep falling back into our old ways and habits, but also how you can prepare yourself for the future. I will suggest the first steps to take during your journey of second chances, give you some questions to ponder, provide conversation starters with those around you, and hopefully leave you in a better state than you are now.

Let's face it: too much is at stake not to go on this journey together. The cost of waiting is too great. You don't need me to tell you that you wish you would have done something earlier. Don't make the same mistake again. The God of Second Chances wants to give you another chance at your marriage, career, family patterns and use you for great things. He knows that your past can't change but your future most certainly can. He also knows that your past has the potential to change someone else's future too.

So, there is no more time to waste. Let's roll up our sleeves and explore together how to move forward after messing up.

For Personal Reflection:

1. Have you ever found yourself asking the questions presented at the beginning of the chapter during challenging moments in your life? What other questions have come to your mind?

2. Consider the idea of second chances. When have you personally experienced or witnessed someone going through a challenging situation, and what would a second chance look like for you and those you love?

For Discussion:

1. Explore the theme of God standing on the shoreline of one's life, ready to offer second chances. How does this perspective influence our understanding of God's grace and the continuous opportunity for a fresh start?

2. In the early stages of this second chance journey, discuss some obstacles and hurdles standing in your way or in the way of your loved one.

3. At the heart of second chances are relationships. Which of your relationships will benefit the most from seeking the God of Second Chances? Share how you want that renewed relationship to look.

FACING WHAT'S REALLY GOING ON

Create in me a pure heart, O God, and renew a steadfast spirit within me.

PSALM 51:10

If you've ever spent time with young children, you know they have a remarkable talent for creating chaos in a matter of minutes.

I'm constantly astounded by the mess my kids can make, even when I turn my back for just a moment. And like any parent, I find myself asking, "What is this you have done?" I can't help but wonder if God felt something similar in the Garden of Eden. God's relationship with His creation was flourishing, and the bond between Him and humanity seemed unbreakable.

However, Adam and Eve underestimated the power of the enemy and the enticement of sin. I am sure Eve did not wake up one morning and say, "Adam, let's make a huge mess of our lives!" But the lure and temptation of sin were in the air, and it was intense. Their choices broke God's heart *and* their relationship with Him. God's final question to them did not reveal His shock, but His genuine love for them: "What is this you have done?" (Genesis 3:13).

I'm sure you didn't wake up one morning and convince yourself to make a mess of your life, either. But somehow, one choice led to another, and you wondered, "What is this I have done?" You journeyed down paths you never thought you would travel. You faced circumstances that were seemingly out of your control. Unfortunately, the past is the past, and there is no turning back. There is no undoing what has already been done. You do not have a giant eraser or delete button that can undo every regrettable decision you've made. But what if I told you about a path forward? It may be a path you never expected, but it is the path you need.

THE REALITY OF A WRECK

"In life, you make decisions, and your decisions, oftentimes, make you."

I don't know how often I heard my mentor say this to me, but it has stuck. Think about your decisions. Odds are you ended up where you are today because of not just one, but a series of choices you (and perhaps others) made. But there is good news. You will face more decisions in your future because God's not done with you yet. In fact, there is a good chance He is just getting started. But first, we have to take inventory and look a little bit closer at the messes in your life, the decisions that led you to where you are, and begin to accurately define your reality.

It was a day that would haunt a nation, a day when tragedy struck the families in Modane, a small town in southeastern France, with a force that would leave its mark forever. On a cold December morning in 1917, a train carried at least a thousand WWI soldiers back home from the front lines to family and friends for the Christmas holiday. Due to a shortage of locomotives, the local commanding officer ordered two trains to be combined into one long train. Even though the train engine was powerful enough to pull the fully loaded nineteen train cars, the engineer was hesitant about the train's ability to brake if needed. Since they were traveling through a mountainous stretch of the Alps in southeastern France, he warned French officials that the hills were too steep for such a heavy load, but he was overruled by the transport officer.

After peeking its head out of a tunnel like a nervous groundhog, the train started to descend from the city of Modane as slowly as possible (6 mph). However, the decision to decline down the mountain had already been made, and disaster was inevitable. The train began accelerating to an eventual uncontrollable speed of 84 mph. The driver applied the brakes, but they failed due to the heavy load. The train derailed, explosions ensued and, because most of the cars were built of wood, the wreck burned, claiming the lives of hundreds of individuals, and leaving behind a wake of destruction and heartache.[1]

The cause of the disaster was rooted in ego, poor decision-making, and a failure to identify the severity of the power of momentum. But in the aftermath of the tragedy, it was clear that this was more than just a simple accident; it was a reminder of the importance of defining what is really going on, how one bad decision can cause us to spiral out of control, and the impact our choices can have on those around us.

Before you can start seeing the light at the end of your tunnel, it is crucial to understand what's really going on. Like Adam, Eve, and God in the Garden of Eden, it's very possible that your relationships with others have suffered because of selfishness and poor decision-making. Whether you realize it or not, your choices have affected your relationships with those closest to you. Your spouse still aches for your companionship. Your kids continue to crave your love. Your siblings long for closeness, and your parents cry out for your affection. It may not seem like it, but there are people who care about you. You matter to them, and you also matter to God. But the mess you find yourself in rips at the fabric of all your relationships.

As I mentioned previously, I have experienced this firsthand. My older brother Nick and I were born less than fifteen months apart. We shared a room throughout childhood and had many similar interests. However, we began to grow apart after our father died when we were in our late teens. Our dad was diagnosed with cancer in March; six months later, he was gone. Nobody teaches you how to handle grief. There isn't one way to mourn. Everybody deals with death on their own terms and in their own way. On the outside, my brother kept the status quo, but inside, you could tell he was heartbroken. We all were.

Our relationship seemed beyond repair.

Nick turned to drugs and alcohol to help him cope. Who could blame him? It was easily accessible and numbed the pain. However, his decisions drove a wedge further between him and me and others in our family. Even though he moved back home with our mom after dropping out of college during his sophomore year, he became increasingly distant from our family. In the years that followed our father's death, whenever I returned home from college, it was like walking on eggshells, knowing that the slightest thing could set Nick off. A small reminder to bring his dishes to the kitchen became a huge ordeal. If I were to change the thermostat one degree, a shouting match would ensue.

Perhaps you have been in a similar situation with a family member. You may not even remember what the argument was about, but you blistered each other with words, and your relationship was never the same. My relationship with my brother seemed beyond repair, as did his relationship with everyone else in our family. I'll tell you more about our story later, so for now, let's focus on you and how you are *really* doing.

YOUR PERSONAL INVENTORY

Before we go any further, it's important to take a moment for self-reflection. Are you truly satisfied with where you are in life right now? Are you content with your relationships, career, and overall well-being? *Really* reflecting on these questions can be a challenging exercise, but it can also provide valuable insights into areas where you may need to focus your attention.

When it comes to relationships, are you giving and receiving love and support in equal measure? Do you feel connected and understood by those around you? Are there tensions and conflicts that need to be addressed? Are some of your relationships just hanging on by a thread? Sometimes it's easy to fall into complacency in our relationships, assuming that they will always be there without putting in the effort to maintain them.

In terms of career, are you finding fulfillment and purpose in your work? Do you feel like you are making a positive impact and contributing to something meaningful? Or are you feeling stuck or unfulfilled in your job, lacking motivation or a sense of purpose? It's normal to experience ups and downs in our careers, but are you so stressed-out that you cannot get through the day without some type of remedy?

Are you enjoying life? Are you making time for activities and experiences that bring you joy and fulfillment, or are you stuck in a rut, going through the motions without truly living? Have you contemplated harming others or yourself?

Asking ourselves these difficult questions can be uncomfortable, but it's an essential step toward growth and fulfillment. It's crucial that we identify the reality of the wreck we are in, the messiness of our lives, and how it has impacted those around us. If you find that you are not satisfied with certain aspects of your life and relationships, it's never too late to make changes and take steps toward a more fulfilling, meaningful, and purpose-filled life.

THE REALITY OF DENIAL

Not too long ago, I noticed a small brown spot on the ceiling above my desk in my home office. I didn't think much of it until a few weeks later, when I glanced up and it apparently had tripled in size. Again, it was still too small for me to waste my time, and besides, I had better things to do. I said to myself, *Maybe it will go away on its own.*

Fast-forward a couple more weeks and imagine bedtime in the Rappazini household with a seven-, five-, and three-year-old. Things are always chaotic at that time in the evening, but of course, this night was one of *those* nights. You know, one of those nights that takes chaos up three notches. This was in large part because my wife was out of town, so it was up to me to put the kids down. In addition to their having angst that Mom was gone, the kids were frightened of the thunder and lightning outside their bedroom windows. Picture me trying to herd not just cats, but scared kittens.

Then all of a sudden, I heard an odd noise coming from my office. I commanded the kids to stay in their rooms and went to investigate. When I entered the room, the situation was easy to diagnose: there was a steady stream of water flowing from those brown spots on the ceiling onto my desk. I quickly ran downstairs, grabbed some small pots, buckets, and towels, and frantically placed them on my desk and the floor. Of course, the kids wanted to see what was happening, and I could feel my blood pressure continuing to rise. After a few moments of reflection, I climbed into the attic with a flashlight, checked the roof, and found the source of the leak. This led me to dash down to the kitchen, grab the largest pot and baking tray I could find, climb back into the attic, and position the tray and pot just right to catch all the water that was coming in from the underside of the roof.

I wish I could say that the next day I climbed onto the roof and fixed the leak, but one thing led to another, and I forgot. Or perhaps a more accurate description is I was in denial that there was even a leak. I mean, the storm was over, water was no longer pouring from the ceiling, my office was dry, so all was well, right? Wrong. Unfortunately, about a month later, another huge storm rolled through our area and caused even more damage than before. Once again, you would think I would call my insurance company, but nope, I was still in denial. I didn't want to face the fact that I needed help. It wasn't until I noticed a roof contractor at a neighbor's house that I was forced to face the reality that my roof, too, needed to be repaired.

Denial serves as a defense mechanism we use to handle harmful situations that threaten our sense of security, control, or comfort. People may choose to ignore the reality of their situations for various reasons, including fear of the truth, lack of awareness, social pressure, or cognitive biases. While denial can temporarily relieve the stress and anxiety of a situation, it can also prevent us from seeking help and finding a solution.

> *God is in the business of cleaning up messes, no matter how big they may seem.*

At some stage in our lives, we have all used denial and excuses, whether it was to skip a workout, avoid a difficult conversation, delay fixing a leaky roof, or address what is really going on. Perhaps lately, though, when it comes to the mess you find yourself in, you have found yourself saying things like:

"Everybody else does it, so why can't I?"

"I'm not hurting anyone else, so what's the problem?"

"I wouldn't need to _____ if my life wasn't so stressful."

"It's not really a problem. I can quit anytime I want, I just don't feel like it right now."

"If only people would listen to me, everything would be fine."

"I'm not addicted, I'm just self-medicating."

"If only that person would hurry up, I could be on my way and get stuff done."

As days go by, you become increasingly frustrated and irritable with people and things. The temptation to make excuses, deny reality, and blame others is strong. But face it, you're tired of the way things are. Deep down, you know something has to change.

The good news is that there is hope for those who are ready to face the truth. God is in the business of cleaning up messes, no matter how big they may seem. But before that can happen, we must first identify the real issue and take responsibility for our actions.

UNDERSTANDING WHAT LIES BENEATH

I'll never forget my first college teaching experience as a professor at the Moody Bible Institute in Spokane, Washington. One of the assignments for my public speaking/preaching students was for them to give a sermon using a visual aid to bring their message to life. (Think of your favorite science teacher using an object to teach the lesson.) Little did I know that one student's sermon introduction would stay with me forever.

Nate walked into the classroom and handed each of us a piece of chocolate. I thought, *What a great start to a sermon; who doesn't love chocolate!?* I could already tell this was going to be memorable. He then asked us to examine the rich shine glimmering off the chocolate. He asked us to put it to our nose and close our eyes. "Before you taste this chocolate, take a moment to smell the deep aromatic fragrance," he suggested. Then he said the words we were all waiting for: "Now, go ahead and take a bite."

However, moments after biting into our chocolate pieces, it dawned on each of us that something was wrong, very wrong. Instead of the chocolate having a sweet taste that excited our taste buds, it was extremely bitter. While we thought we were about to enjoy a piece of milk chocolate, we were caught off guard because what we were nibbling on was *baking chocolate*, which has a very bitter taste.

We rapidly reached for our napkins and bottled water to quickly get the awful taste out of our mouths. After a few more moments of us smacking our mouths in disgust, Nate told us the point he was trying to make: "The baking chocolate appeared delicious, but it turned out to be repulsive. Similarly, sin often looks so good, but it often has a bitter bite." He went on to explain the story between King David and Bathsheba in 2 Samuel 11. Let me give you a quick recap of what happened, as it will shed light on helping us identify the real issue you're dealing with.

David was the king of Israel. His army was at war. He was supposed to be with his fellow soldiers in battle. Instead, he was at home on his rooftop balcony in Jerusalem. Looking out at his vast territory, he noticed someone on another rooftop below. It was a woman. But not just any woman—it was a very attractive and alluring woman. And she was bathing. At first, he glanced away because he was a man of God. But then he couldn't resist. What started with a quick glance turned into a classic case of "rooftop romance research." Then, he remembered that he was the most powerful man in all of Israel. He could have whatever he desired, including her. So, he commanded his agents to bring her to him. This decision was only the beginning of his troubles.

You can read more details in 2 Samuel 11, but spoiler alert, David got her pregnant. He quickly ordered her husband, Uriah, to return from the war, thinking he would naturally sleep with his wife. That would surely cover up what David had done. Instead, Uriah refused to sleep with his wife and begged David to allow him to go back to war because of his desire to serve his nation (*cough-cough*, like David should have been doing all along). King David sent Uriah back into battle and ordered him to be placed where the battle was the heaviest, and eventually Uriah was killed.

If we are going to talk about what's really going on, we have to address the issue of sin.

David's deceptive scheme worked. Uriah was finally out of the picture, and David was now unhindered to marry Bathsheba. From the outside looking in, David was the compassionate king looking after a pregnant widow. But the reality was that one poor decision led to the next, and calamity fell on him and those around him. Sadly, the child born to them only lived a week (2 Samuel 12:18). What a mess! David didn't just take a bite of the baking chocolate; he ate the whole bar. At first, seeing Bathsheba on that rooftop looked good, but eventually, he learned that sin has a very bitter bite.

So, what does David, Bathsheba, and chocolate have to do with you? The predicament you find yourself in is because of the internal condition within each one of us. It's called sin. I recognize "sin" is a very religious word, but face it, even though sin looks good, it has a bitter bite. If we are going to talk about what's really going on, we have to address the issue of sin. When we look at the story of David and Bathsheba, we think the problem is his pride, lust, or selfishness. But those aren't the problems at all. Those are simply cover-ups for what is really going on. The main issue is his internal condition of sin.

Many of us believe that our problems stem from drugs, alcohol, lust, greed, or whatever other issues we're dealing with. But these actually only offer short-term alleviation to our deeper internal condition. They are how we try to cope with our inner turmoil caused by sin. This may be why you have tried to make changes in the past, but nothing ever stuck. You were never able to identify the root of it all, sin. David's story serves as a cautionary tale. He tried to solve his internal struggles his way, but in the end, his choices were temporary fixes that only made things worse. The real issue going on was his condition of sin.

PROBLEMS AND CONDITIONS

Understanding the difference between a *problem* and a *condition* is crucial. Problems generally have straightforward solutions, whereas conditions require ongoing effort to manage and eventually overcome. A broken finger or the flu is a problem that can be overcome with medicine and time. Chronic back pain or diabetes, on the other hand, are examples of a condition that is monitored and needs much more time and focus. Our inner turmoil is beyond a problem; it is a condition of sin that requires extensive work. Perhaps this is why you have been stuck in a rut as long as you have been. You have been treating your problem and not your condition. You have been using a Band-Aid when a serious surgical operation is needed. But by recognizing our true condition, we can seek the help we need to find the peace we desire.

Where does that leave us? Better yet, where does that leave you? It leaves you with a choice: to either continue down your path, follow your own ways, and keep trying to remedy your problems with quick fixes and the latest life hacks, or acknowledge your true condition called sin, allow the Great Healer to give you what you need to move forward, and follow Him down the path He wants to lead you. The choice is up to you.

ONE DECISION AT A TIME

I've heard about a house in the Midwest where rain droplets that fall on one side of the roof flow through a downspout into a river that eventually runs into the north Atlantic Ocean. The droplets that fall on the other side of the roof flow into a river that leads into the Gulf of Mexico. Just a mere gust of wind can change the destination of a single raindrop. This house serves as a powerful reminder that even the smallest choices we make can have a profound impact on our ultimate destination.[2]

In Luke 7:36–50, we find a woman whose life was transformed by one decision. A very similar one that you may be facing. Do I continue on my path, or do I choose the way Jesus wants to lead me? Luke doesn't record her name and only describes her as the one who regularly sins (vv. 37, 39). She was most likely known throughout the community for her bad reputation. Can you envision how people would have stared at her when she walked down the streets? Imagine how she would have felt every time insults were hurled at her.

Her life was in shambles. But when she heard that Jesus was in town, she had to see Him. Unlike other men who most likely had taken advantage of her, Jesus was the only one offering genuine peace and true rest. Joe Stowell surmises that it is very likely that earlier that day, she had heard Jesus preaching and say, "Come to me, all you who are weary and burdened, and I will give you rest. Take my yoke upon you and learn from me, for I am gentle and humble in heart, and you will find rest for your souls" (Matthew 11:28–30).[3] For some reason, she couldn't get those words out of her head and couldn't get Jesus off her mind. So that night, she decided to crash a Pharisee's party, get close to Jesus, and do something that people are still talking about today.

With great boldness and courage, she located where Jesus was dining that evening and entered the house of Simon the Pharisee. Kneeling behind Jesus, she was emotionally moved. Her passionate tears began to fall on Jesus' feet, and she proceeded to wipe His feet with her hair and pour the expensive perfume she brought on His head.

It is important to know that in first-century Judaism, when someone entered a house for a meal, the host would greet everyone with a kiss and supply water to clean their dirty feet. The host would then provide oil or perfume for everyone in preparation for the meal. It would be similar today when a dinner host takes a guest's coat, shakes hands, and sets the table in preparation for the meal. However, when Jesus entered Simon's house, none of that happened. Instead of being hospitable, Simon, the law-lover, though curious, was skeptical and cynical of Jesus and His ministry. But this woman was moved to make a decision. She literally took one small courageous step after another toward Jesus.

The moment she opened her perfume bottle, its aroma filled the room. This was probably the last straw for Simon the Pharisee. Upon seeing what was happening under his roof, he started fuming. He muttered under his breath, "If this man were a prophet, he would know . . ." (Luke 7:39). Luke tells us that Jesus then turned to the Pharisee and said,

"Simon, I have something to tell you. . . . Two people owed money to a certain moneylender. One owed him five hundred denarii, and the other fifty. Neither of them had the money to pay him back, so he forgave the debts of both. Now which of them will love him more?" (vv. 40–42)

Simon answered correctly, "I suppose the one who had the bigger debt forgiven." Turning and looking at the woman, Jesus spoke to Simon,

"Do you see this woman? I came into your house. *You* did not give me any water for my feet, but *she* wet my feet with her tears and wiped them with her hair. *You* did not give me a kiss, but *this woman*, from the time I entered, has not stopped kissing my feet. *You* did not put oil on my head, but *she* has poured perfume on my feet. Therefore, I tell you, her many sins have been forgiven—as her great love has shown. But whoever has been forgiven little loves little." Then Jesus said to her, "Your sins are forgiven." (Luke 7:44–48)

The night she decided to see Jesus and express her emotions marked a pivotal moment in her life. Until then, she had been caught in a cycle of poor choices, where one misstep led to another. However, with one small decision to take a step toward Jesus, her life was forever transformed.

What better time is there to seek God than when we are weakened by our sin? Like King David and like this woman who cried at Jesus' feet, we are broken sinners and in need of help with our internal condition. Help with what is *really* going on. We cannot do it on our own, and we need Him. We must make the decision to pursue Him one small step at a time.

SO, NOW WHAT?

One of my all-time favorite movies is *Back to the Future*, which I loved as a child and still enjoy today. (I know it is a little dated, but allow me to reminisce about the glory days of the 80s and 90s for a moment.) Who wouldn't want to befriend a wacky scientist and travel through time in a DeLorean? Just picture opening those iconic vertical doors, pushing some buttons, and being transported to a different era where you could alter the course of your life and those of others. It would be amazing! However, the reality is that while you may know a few eccentric people in your neighborhood, you cannot change the past or erase what's already happened. But you can change your future one small decision at a time.

The choice is up to you. You can keep going your route and try to manage your addiction. You can maintain the status quo with your marriage, job, life, and so on, but I'm confident you can do better than just get by with the current state of affairs. I'm not promising you will have the future you always wanted, but I can promise you that you can have the future God wants for you. A future full of second chances.

So, now that we know that what is really going on is our internal condition of sin and how our decisions make and shape us, don't stop now. Keep moving forward toward your future by getting to know more about the One who wants to take you there.

For Personal Reflection

1. How have your actions and choices affected your relationships with family, friends, and loved ones? Are there any specific instances that stand out to you?
2. In what ways have you attempted to cope with your internal turmoil caused by sin, and how have these coping mechanisms affected your journey toward recovery?

For Discussion

1. The chapter emphasizes the importance of recognizing our internal condition of sin. How do you understand the concept of sin in your life, and how has it contributed to your struggles?
2. Denial is a common defense mechanism in addiction. Have you ever experienced denial in your journey forward? If so, what steps can you take to face the truth and seek help?
3. The chapter encourages making one small decision at a time to change your future. What small steps can you take in your journey to move toward the future God wants for you? How can a supportive community, such as a church recovery group, friends to hold you accountable, or rehab program, help in this process?

THE GOD OF
SECOND CHANCES

> For God so loved the world that he gave his one and
> only Son, that whoever believes in him shall not perish
> but have eternal life.
> **JOHN 3:16**

When you think about "God," what comes to mind? Is it a Zeus-like character etched in stone? Does He look like the magnificent figure who is depicted on the ceiling of the Sistine Chapel? Maybe you picture a light-skinned man in a white robe, with shoulder-length, brownish-blonde hair, and wearing sandals. Perhaps at your core, you wonder if God is even real. Regardless of what you believe at this moment, what comes to your mind when you think about God is the most important thing you can ever consider.[4]

If you think you can just write God off or put the question of God on the back burner on your road to recovery, think again. If you are skeptical about God, you are not alone. In this chapter, I want to introduce you to others who raise some great questions about God, including me. But let's not stop with asking questions, let's seek some answers. Now, you may be wondering, why do I need to know about God on my path to healing? What does He have to do with anything?

Well, the only way to overcome your internal condition of sin, which is the root cause of what is really going on, is to turn to the only one who has ever truly defeated sin. If you want to see lasting change, the kind that truly has the power to transform your life, then we have to turn to someone who has everlasting power. Learning more about God will answer the questions of what second chances look like, why and when He offers them, and how we can really move forward after messing up. So, strap yourself in, because before we can go any further in your second chance, we need to learn more about the God of Second Chances.

"SOMETHING BIGGER GOING ON"

Imagine strolling down a busy street in the heart of a bustling city when you spot something strange. At first, you see one person recklessly running down the middle of the road, seemingly undeterred by the danger of traffic. You assume they must be crazy, and you quickly dismiss them as just another eccentric city dweller. But then, as you keep walking, you notice two more people running down the middle of the road, and then ten more, and even more after that. You can't help but wonder, *Is there something bigger going on here than I first thought?*

As you stop to take a closer look, you realize that they're all dressed in running gear and have bibs with numbers pinned to their shirts. You start to see the situation in a new light. These people aren't irrational, they're participating in a marathon (okay, maybe they are still a little crazy for running 26.2 miles). What you initially thought was madness was actually a well-organized event.

This experience serves as a reminder that our perspectives can shape our understanding of the world, and it's important to keep an open mind as we think about the existence of God. Before dismissing the notion of a personal God who cares about you, consider taking a closer look and giving yourself the opportunity to understand the bigger picture.

We all have an idea of God. Even if you don't believe or aren't sure He exists, that is *still* an idea about God. Sure, it would be easy if each of us could make up our own ideas about God, concluding something like "As long as I'm sincere" or "Whatever you believe, if it's good for you, it's fine with me." But this reasoning doesn't really hold up. You and I can make up whatever we wanted to about God, but that wouldn't mean it was true. You and I have only a minimal scope of this world. So it's vital to explore who God truly is and not rely solely on our limited perspective because something bigger might be going on.

GOD'S DIVINE NATURAL ATTRIBUTES

The Swiss chemist Johann Friedrich Miescher first identified the molecule now known as DNA in the 1860s. Over the next hundred years, scientists learned that DNA contains the essential instructions for an organism to develop, survive, and reproduce. In other words, DNA tells the genetic makeup of every living creature. If you look deep enough, our DNA tells the story of why our bodies are the way they are. To discover what your DNA says about you, someone would need to take a sample of your DNA, run it through a lab creating thousands of pages of results, and then an expert would interpret the results for you.

The Bible is a way of looking at the general makeup of God. It is like reading and interpreting the results of God's DNA. It tells the story of who He is and what He is like. Perhaps we could think of the Scriptures as telling us God's DNA, His Divine Natural Attributes.

So, if we are on a journey to figure out who God is and what He is like, it is crucial to look at His divine natural attributes as He revealed to us in the Bible.

Several of these divine natural attributes quickly come to mind. For instance, in His general makeup, we would find that God is powerful, and nothing can stand in His way. In Jeremiah 32:27, He says, "I am the LORD, the God of all mankind. Is anything too hard for me?" God is limitless in His power. There is nothing and no one more powerful than He is. If there were, then He wouldn't be the true God. There is no limitation to God's power.

Another characteristic of God's divine natural attributes is His holiness. In other words, God is holy and set apart from sin. He is entirely different from us and wants nothing to do with sin, yet everything to do with us. He is "other" and transcends this sinful world. The Israelites sang, "Who among the gods is like you, O LORD? Who is like you—majestic in holiness, awesome in glory, working wonders?" (Exodus 15:11).

In the Bible, we would also find that what makes God indeed God is that He is eternal. God is not limited by time, as He exists at all points in the past and future. A. W. Tozer says, "The mind looks backward in time till the dim past vanishes, then turns and looks into the future till thought and imagination collapse from exhaustion: and God is at both points, unaffected by either."[5] Moses writes, "Before the mountains were born or you brought forth the world, from everlasting to everlasting you are God" (Psalm 90:2). There has never been a time when God did not exist, and there will never be a time when He does not exist.

We could continue to look at other attributes that make up God's DNA, including His justice, mercy, omniscience, wisdom, and sovereignty, but one component that can be so easily overlooked is that second chances are part of God's DNA too. You won't find a "Second Chances" section in any theology textbook. Perhaps that is because it may sound too similar to God's grace or forgiveness, but God's DNA of second chances goes further, because it includes you. God could not be graceful unless there was someone to extend grace to. He could not be forgiving unless someone needed forgiveness. And God could not be the God of Second Chances without you.

WHY DOES GOD GIVE SECOND CHANCES?

Have you ever wondered, "Why does God even give people multiple chances?" Or maybe another way to think about it is, if somebody is so messed up, why would God even spend time helping them get back on their feet? Why doesn't He move on to someone who's got their life together? With eight billion people on earth, doesn't God have enough people to choose from? Is He so desperate for people to follow Him that He goes after those most in need and vulnerable?

You could also ask, "Why does God give second chances at all? Can't He be doing something better and more productive? Wouldn't He rather spend time floating around on clouds and creating breathtaking sunsets, all the while being serenaded by angels with harps? Why would God want to waste His time showing up at a rehab center? Why would he care about someone's spending habits or anger issues? Why would He spend His Friday nights hanging out at an AA meeting?"

Odd gods: While it may seem obvious to us now, many people throughout history couldn't make sense of the idea that there is only one God who gives people multiple chances. Throughout history, many cultures have worshiped false gods who demand respect out of fear, terror, and the threat of consequences. The ancient Greeks, for example, had several gods who were to be worshiped out of fear rather than love. They thought that Poseidon would drown your boat if you disrespected the sea, and Apollo, the god of the sun, would send plagues on your family or community if you forgot to sacrifice to him. Even neglecting your craft or producing shoddy work for Athena, the goddess of wisdom, war, and crafts, could result in losing your skill or creativity altogether.

It is not just the ancient Greeks who lived in fear and terror of their gods. The Egyptians had Ra, the god of the sun; Anubis, the god of the dead; and Isis, the goddess of motherhood and fertility. The Hindus have Brahma, the god of creation; Vishnu, the god of preservation and protection; and Shiva, the god of destruction and regeneration. Each of these cultures have multiple gods that emphasize everything except unconditional love.

A different viewpoint: In contrast, the Bible presents a different story: the story of one God, Yahweh, who loves unconditionally. But even many of those who studied the Scriptures and the ways of Yahweh closely, the Pharisees, missed that God was a loving God.

A few Pharisees around the time of Jesus wanted to dig a bit deeper into the mystery of God's love. You see, the Pharisees were the best of the best when it came to following the commands of the Torah, the first five books of the Old Testament. People turned to these religious scholars for answers to their theological questions. Their full-time job was essentially being good and obedient to the religious laws. But many Pharisees and other experts in the law hated Jesus. They hated what He taught. They hated that He didn't keep their rules as they thought He should. Mostly they hated that people started to listen and follow Him instead of them. But that didn't stop

Jesus from showing the world that God is a God who loves everyone.

But there was a small group of Pharisees who thought that maybe, just maybe, God was up to something at that moment. They wondered if it were possible that Jesus was actually from God and that the message that "God is love" was true.

We don't know how it all transpired, but this small group of Pharisees got together early one morning and decided they had to get some answers from Jesus Himself. They didn't understand all His teachings, but they had witnessed Him do miraculous things. They couldn't explain what they saw, but they knew something was different about Him. He knew so much about the Scriptures, but the way He talked and interacted with others was inviting and compassionate.

This small sect of Pharisee radicals weren't ready to follow Him as God's Son, the promised Messiah, but they couldn't ignore Him, either. They particularly had one question they needed to ask Jesus. So, they decided that Nicodemus was the perfect guy to approach Jesus because he was the Pharisee who was one of the oldest, wisest, and closest to being perfect. Nicodemus didn't want the anti-Jesus Pharisees to know what he was doing, so he found a time at night and met with Jesus unnoticed.

Jesus said that God's love, not one's way of life, is the determining factor for second chances.

Under the cover of darkness, Nicodemus found Jesus and began asking Him the question he had probably been rehearsing the whole way over. But Jesus did that thing that He often did. He answered someone's question before it was even asked. Before Nicodemus could open his mouth, Jesus said, "Very truly I tell you, no one can see the kingdom of God unless they are born again" (John 3:3). Several thoughts probably ran through Nicodemus' mind: *How on earth can someone be born again? What does that even mean? I wanted to talk about God's love, not rebirth.*

Jesus explained a bit more, but I'll speed ahead for us. Here's the summary of God's intent, birthed in love:

For God so loved the world that he gave his one and only Son, that whoever believes in him shall not perish but have eternal life. For God did not send his Son into the world to condemn the world, but to save the world through him. (John 3:16–17)

Did you catch that? I'm not sure if Nicodemus did either, at least not at first. Jesus said that God's love, not one's way of life, is the determining factor for second chances. Eternal life is possible because "God so loved the world."

For Nicodemus, it was too overwhelming. He grew up, perhaps like you did, learning that God was always looking at him the same way a 1960s authoritarian schoolteacher would target misbehaving students. You know the type—the one with eyes in the back of their head and a knack for catching mischief from a mile away. If you behaved, you stayed out of trouble, but if you misbehaved, you were sent to the principal's office and punished. Nicodemus learned in Pharisee school that if you want a right standing with God and wish to have eternal life with Him, you must be able to keep God's commandments as much as possible. But the slightest misstep resulted in God handing you an eternal detention slip.

Jesus threw Nicodemus a curveball when He said that whoever *believes* will have eternal life. To which Nicodemus probably thought, *Wait, Jesus. Don't you mean whoever behaves will have eternal life?* But Jesus didn't misspeak; He's the author of truth, after all. It has nothing to do with proper behavior. Instead, it is an internal thing. It has everything to do with what one believes.

Explain that again. But why would God allow anyone, regardless of background and conduct, to have eternal life with Him? Why would God give everyone, everywhere, the possibility for a do-over? Simply put, because "God so loved the world."

God's love for the world is something that we will never fully comprehend. We can sense it. We can see a glimpse of it in how a parent loves their child, but God's unconditional love for you and me will be something we will spend all of eternity trying to understand and only begin to scratch the surface. God does not gain anything by having us. Instead, it turns out it is the complete opposite. We gain everything by having Him. But for this to happen, He had to lose everything. God showcased His love when He sent His one and only Son into the world so that we might live through Him (1 John 4:8–10).

The reason why God gives second chances to people like you, me, and my brother will always be beyond us. It surely isn't because God needs us, as He is all-sufficient. Surely, He is not bored, since He is the Creator of all things. So then, why *does* God give us second chances? In a word: love. There is no other way to explain why God offers second chances than He is a God who loves.

The only word that can summarize why God gives us second chances is *love.*

WHEN DOES GOD GIVE SECOND CHANCES?

A few years ago, while playing flag football with some college-age students, during the final play of the game, I made a dive for a pass that ended up being a costly mistake. Not only did I miss the catch, but in the process, I cracked some ribs, leaving me in agony for weeks. My once mundane routines around the house became a test of endurance as even the simple acts of sleeping, laughing, or moving became a source of intense pain. However, as my ribs eventually healed, I was reminded of two valuable lessons. First, I realized that I was not as young and invincible as I thought, and second, physical injuries have the power to completely debilitate our lives.

It must have been both exhilarating and frustrating to be one of Jesus' disciples. On the one hand, they got a front-row seat to the miracle worker Himself. Every morning they awoke to wonder whom the Messiah might heal that day. Who would be set free from their physical ailment? After one encounter with Jesus, paralytics could stroll through the marketplace. The deaf heard the birds chirping in the distance. The blind could finally see the sun reflect off the radiant colors of the sea for the first time. And, if Jesus wanted, all of this could happen before breakfast.

On the other hand, the disciples scratched their heads, wondering why Jesus chose to heal some but not all. Why did He pass through the town square and not touch all those who reached out? Why did He seemingly ignore the cries and coughs of some of the sick? Did He have to be in the right mood for a healing touch?

Perhaps the disciples thought Jesus' miraculous mulligans were given at random or to a select few. When exactly does God give second chances? To explore this question, let's take a closer look at when Jesus gave a second chance in a way that was not what anyone expected.

Jesus' unexpected words: For some friends of a paralyzed man, they were willing to roll the dice to see if Jesus would give their friend another opportunity at a healthier life. In Capernaum, possibly at the home of the apostle Peter, the friends of the paralytic could not get into the crowded house where Jesus was teaching. So, they climbed the outside stairs, made a hole in the mud and straw roof, and carefully lowered their friend like precious cargo on a freight elevator to get him in front of the Great Healer (Mark 2:1–4). What determination! Nothing would stand in their way of getting their disabled friend in front of Jesus. Not a crowd, not a roof, nothing.

Despite their efforts, Jesus' first words were not what they sought. They were probably anticipating something along the lines of, "Behold and watch, as I work some magic and cure your buddy!" Instead, they heard, "Son, your sins are forgiven" (Mark 2:5). This makeshift medical team wanted their friend to be physically healed, not to be forgiven of his sins! However, little did they know that even though Jesus' words were not what they had come for, they were exactly what was needed.

Jesus came to the world to be more than a physical healer. Jesus came at just the right time to give people another chance with God. From the beginning, Jesus was on a rescue mission. He was not just concerned about healing people's bodies, but about

God gives second chances when people are ready to accept Him.

saving their souls. He came to help people move forward by setting them free from their sins. Jesus gives second chances at just the right time, often when we least expect it. To solidify His authority to forgive sins, He also healed people physically. That is what He did for the paralyzed man. But even though his elevator-crew friends wanted him to be able to walk again, the real miracle had already been done. Jesus gave a sinner's soul a second chance that would last for all eternity.

This is just one of many examples Jesus gives to teach us that God gives us second chances when people are ready to accept Him.

God does not give second chances to people haphazardly. He does not wake up every morning, spin a gigantic lottery wheel of everyone's name, and give second chances to that day's "winner." He knows what everyone needs and precisely when they need it. He knew that those friends would bring the paralytic. He knew exactly who would be watching. God extends second chances at just the right time and in just the right way.

God does the same for you and me too. If you think He's not paying attention and doesn't see your pain, you're wrong. It doesn't matter how far you have strayed from Him. He offers us a second chance at the very moment when we need it the most, when we are ready to accept Him.

Perhaps He is doing that right now. It looks different for everyone, but He has placed you where you are today for a purpose. As Jesus said Himself, those who need a second chance the most are the ones who have strayed the farthest. You may think, "Well, don't I need to stop smoking, find a job, and control my anger issues? Don't I need to figure out my direction in life, complete rehab, or get out of jail before I can follow Jesus and start moving forward?" The short answer is no. Just like you don't clean up before you take a shower, you don't need to clean up your life before you start following Jesus. Your second chance could be right now.

"FINALLY, THE SECOND CHANCE HE NEEDED"

My brother Nick spent several weeks in jail awaiting trial after being charged with several misdemeanors and a felony. However, his struggles started long before his arrest. Addictive tendencies run in our family, and he was no exception. As much as he thought he could handle his alcohol and other addictions, the law said otherwise.

The courts move at the pace of a sloth on tranquilizers, so it was no surprise that there were delays at every turn while he awaited his trial. Since Nick had been arrested and was in jail at the end of November and into December, it just seemed like there was one delay after another, especially with the surrounding holidays. I lived on the other side of the country, so I kept my phone close by, waiting for his random fifteen-minute collect calls from jail.

Every time he called, he'd tell me how his cellmates were loud and the food was lousy. It was hard to hear him talk about such a bleak existence when I knew how independent he used to be. Back when he was a sous-chef at a fancy restaurant in New Orleans, he was living the life. But now, he was stuck in a cell with nothing but time and his thoughts.

I'll admit, I was relieved when he didn't ask me to bail him out. That would have been a tough decision to make. But it was still hard knowing he'd be spending the holidays behind bars. At least he was safe there, and he wouldn't hurt anyone or himself.

Nick gave me the names of his public defender and counselor who were helping him with his case, and I reached out to them to learn what the next steps would be. Everybody involved knew Nick needed to go to rehab, not just for a few days, but for a few months, if not longer. Well, everybody knew it, except Nick. His trial continued to get delayed for various reasons, but thankfully the judge allowed him to be admitted to a 28-day Intensive Residential Treatment (IRT) program while he awaited trial.

For Nick, anything was better than the jail cell where he had been for over two months, so he quickly agreed. When we spoke on the phone after his arrival at rehab, he was pleased to be there instead of jail. It was the last phone call he was allowed to have before beginning his 28 days of rehab. Since he was previously homeless and had very few possessions, I vigorously wrote down the basic supplies he needed so I could send him care packages. We said our goodbyes and, after hanging up the phone, I thought, *Finally, the second chance he needed.* He was then given another opportunity after his 28-day IRT was over to move into another program for three months. Things seemed to be looking up. Nick was finally getting the second chances he needed, or so we thought.

Unfortunately, with only a few days left to go in his three-month rehabilitation, he was kicked out of the center for various reasons. Someone had stolen his laptop, and when he tried to get it back, he was charged with assault. We had all thought that by completing the terms of the rehabilitation, he would find favor with the judge, and the charges would be dropped. But now, he was worse off than when he started. The words never came out of our mouths, but we all wondered, "Did he just blow his second chance with the judge and his future?"

WHAT DOES A SECOND CHANCE LOOK LIKE?

You may have wondered what your second chances look like. They are different for everyone and can take many different forms, depending on the situation and context. A second chance may involve a judge and jury. It may include family and friends. It may comprise a new relationship or career. Or, in the case of the woman caught in adultery in John 8, a second chance could mean an entire transformation, brought about by a life-changing encounter with the God of Second Chances.

One more story and then I'll close out this chapter. First, picture the scene. As Jesus is teaching near the temple, a woman is brought before Him and forced to stand in the center of the crowd. Likely she drops her head, expecting to be condemned by the man known by some as the great teacher of Galilee. Jesus looks down at her, His piercing gaze seeing through the veil of her past and into her soul. He already knows the truth about the accusations that have led her to this moment. The air is thick with tension as the Pharisees and teachers of the law circled around, their sharp eyes seeking to trap Jesus with their inquiries. They question Jesus as to what they should do with this adulteress.

The woman felt shame and embarrassment for being caught in adultery and dragged in front of Jesus. What she thought she and her lover were doing in secret had now been exposed to the whole community. The religious leaders had turned their backs on her, and her family would soon disown her if they hadn't already.

Now in the presence of the Pharisees and Jesus, she was simply being used by those who held more power than she did. She was a pawn in the Pharisees' chess game with Jesus. If He let her go, He would be disobeying the Mosaic law. But if He allowed her to be executed, not only would that be a harsh and cruel death, but Jesus would be defying the Roman government, who had taken the right of carrying out capital punishment away from the Jews.

However, unlike the Pharisees, Jesus saw her for who she truly was: someone who mattered. Even though she probably felt that nobody cared about her, she was significant to the God of Second Chances.

With stones in their hands, the Pharisees and teachers of the law anxiously anticipated Jesus' verdict. Would she get the death sentence, or would He and His ministry be considered fraudulent? After a few brief moments during which He bent down and wrote "on the ground with his finger" (v. 6), Jesus responded to the crowd with a simple yet convicting statement, "Let any one of *you* who is without sin be the first to throw a stone at *her*" (John 8:7). After a fleeting moment of silence, thud. Then another, thud. Stones dropped to the ground one by one, and the accusers dispersed.

According to the Mosaic law, two or more witnesses of a crime are required for a person to get the death penalty. Now, all the witnesses were gone. The only one left in the woman's presence was Jesus. He could now release her and still obey the Mosaic law. She was now free and walked away, realizing that she was more than just an object. Her life mattered, and it mattered to Jesus.

Could you imagine having to air your secret acts before a crowd, let alone Jesus? It is often difficult to sift through our world's competing messages about us. Too often, society tells us we are not good enough, pretty enough, or intelligent enough to matter and receive a second chance. But here's the truth: no matter how far you may have strayed, you hold immense value in the eyes of God. He yearns for you to come to Him, bringing your messy and flawed life. Rest assured: He will embrace you with open arms so you can move forward. To God, second chances are a crucial aspect of His character because He views every person as invaluable and precious. In His eyes, you are a priceless gem worthy of love, compassion, and forgiveness.

What do second chances look like? They are different for each of us and take many different forms. But there is one common denominator in every second chance: a person like you. Every second chance consists of a person whom God highly values.

Moving forward after messing up doesn't have to be a daunting or mysterious task. The God of Second Chances is always there, eagerly waiting to offer you a fresh start and a new path. Perhaps you've been searching for a path forward in all the wrong places, but the truth is, He's been waiting for you all along. The God of Second Chances is the ultimate source of compassion and grace, giving second chances with great joy, precisely at the right moment. So, if you're ready to start fresh, come to the God of Second Chances. Embrace the opportunity to begin again, and let His love help guide you toward a life filled with hope and purpose. As we will see in the next chapter, maybe He has already been doing that for years.

For Personal Reflection

1. Consider the analogy of God's DNA as revealed through the Scriptures. Are there specific Bible verses or stories that resonate with you and your journey, and why?
2. How has your understanding of God's love and second chances influenced the way you view yourself and others around you? How do you see the potential for second chances in your future?

For Discussion

1. Share with others if your perception of God has changed recently, and why or why not. What factors contributed to these changes, and how have they impacted your journey?
2. Discuss the concept of unconditional love as demonstrated by God in giving second chances. How does this understanding affect the way you view yourself and others who may be struggling with moving forward?
3. Share your thoughts on the scene with the woman caught in adultery and Jesus' response. How does this story emphasize the value and worth that God places on every individual, regardless of their past?

FROM SETBACKS TO STEPPING STONES

My grace is sufficient for you, for my power is made perfect in weakness.

2 CORINTHIANS 12:9

Have you ever wondered why some people seem to be able to move forward while others don't?

Do you sometimes think that redemption stories are only for the privileged few? Perhaps you've read or heard stories of individuals who have overcome insurmountable odds and experienced miraculous transformations. You can't help but feel a tinge of envy or disbelief. But here's the truth: everyone can move forward after messing up. It's a common misconception that only those who deserve second chances or those who are young enough to benefit from them can receive a fresh start. The reality is that everyone deserves a new beginning, no matter the severity of their mistakes, their age, or any other factors.

It's not uncommon to see famous or newsworthy individuals being praised for their comebacks. We see how they've rebuilt their careers and personal lives through hard work, perseverance, and support. We might be tempted to believe that do-overs are only for those with access to resources and opportunities. However, that couldn't be further from the truth. The most meaningful and transformative renewal stories often happen in the lives of everyday people like you and me.

AN EVERYDAY DIFFERENCE MAKER

Peter grew up in Rockford, a suburb just outside of Chicago. His dad was a pastor and his mother made sure he and his sisters were in church every time the doors were open. But there was a bit of a rebellious streak in Peter, and when he was a teenager, he would go to church on Sunday, but he made Monday through Saturday all about experimenting with every type of drug he could get his hands on. After barely graduating from high school, he enrolled at a nearby community college, but every day was all about trying to live "the life." Or so he thought.

His parents sat back and observed how Peter was throwing his life away. Since his dad was familiar with the Moody Bible Institute in downtown Chicago, they gave Peter an ultimatum: either apply to go to school at Moody or move out of the house and be on your own. Not wanting to be homeless, Peter filled out the application, fabricating most of the material, and never believing he would actually be accepted. Which he wasn't, at first. After being wait-listed for months, a room in the dorm opened up the day before classes began; Peter was offered the last spot and he accepted.

That night he had a deep, heartfelt conversation . . . with God. In his family driveway, he shared with God his fears and anxieties as well as his need for Him in his life. He gave his life to Christ and took one small step toward his new future. The next day, his parents drove him to the campus of Moody Bible Institute in Chicago, all but left the car engine running, and dropped him off at orientation.

Day after day, week after week, and semester after semester, the Lord worked in his life. Peter built tremendous friendships and deep relationships with the guys in his dorm as he witnessed what a life of following Jesus looked like and how the grace of God has no limits. During his time at Bible college, God gave Peter a passion for spreading the gospel and making disciples and Peter never looked back.

Nearly thirty years later, Peter is still using his story of his past to change others' futures. I remember first hearing his story decades ago, when I was a teenager in his youth group. As my youth pastor growing up, Peter discipled me, and was a primary reason I felt called into ministry and went to college at the Moody Bible Institute. He also sat with me when I was a teenager and found out my father died and stood beside me a decade later at my wedding. Few people have impacted my life more than he has. It's everyday people like Peter who are the difference makers in the world because they use their setbacks as stepping stones not just for themselves, but for others around them.

It's easy to get caught up in the misconceptions perpetuated by movies and novels, where characters like George Bailey in *It's a Wonderful Life* or Andy Dufresne in *The Shawshank Redemption* get another opportunity at life through conveniently timed interventions or Hollywood plot twists. But life isn't a movie, and no angels are showing up at our doorsteps to offer us a fresh start. However, that doesn't mean that second chances are out of reach for us.

Recognizing that moving forward after messing up is not limited to only famous or newsworthy individuals or found solely in fiction novels or movies is essential to stepping into our second chances. Everyone deserves the opportunity to learn from their mistakes and grow, regardless of their public profile or background. In fact, if you keep reading, you may be able to identify the second chances God has already given you and how to rely on Him more in the future. Let's explore the Scriptures to open our eyes to the multiple opportunities God has already provided for us everyday people, and learn to appreciate them as the stepping stones to a brighter future for us and others.

THE LEAST LIKELY

Ray Lewis, the legendary football player known for his ferocity on the field, also had a tumultuous personal life. Despite winning two Super Bowls and MVP awards, he was indicted on charges of aggravated assault and murder. But in the midst of his downward spiral, Lewis turned to God and began following Jesus, finding the fresh start he needed.[6]

When Jesus began His earthly ministry, He sought people like Lewis. Not necessarily Hall of Fame football players with notoriety. Or even those who were wealthy and wielded power. Instead, Jesus sought men and women who were in need of a change and a second chance but didn't know where to find it.

Jesus invited uneducated, rough-around-the-edges fishermen to follow in His footsteps. He called women who were victims of sexual assault to join His movement for change. Even political extremists followed Jesus in hopes that they would one day storm the Jerusalem palace compound and overthrow the Roman government. But perhaps the most surprising of all whom Jesus welcomed into His inner circle were the tax collectors, despite their less-than-stellar reputation.

Instead of working for the people, these first-century tax collectors were Jews who worked for Rome. Along with charging an absurd amount of taxes to their Jewish brothers and sisters to pay for the Roman Emperor's wish list, they were allowed to pad their own pockets as much as they wanted. Imagine how surprised Jesus' disciples were when Matthew, a notorious tax collector in Judea, was invited to join the group and follow Him too.

Matthew describes his first encounter with Jesus by writing in third person. "As Jesus went on from there, he saw a man named Matthew sitting at the tax collector's booth. 'Follow me,' he told him, and Matthew got up and followed him" (Matthew 9:9). Two words did it for him. Matthew didn't need a sermon or a miracle—just the calm, inviting tone of Jesus' words, "Follow me." That moment was branded on his memory. Sitting in that tax collector's booth, he recognized he needed something more from those passing by than just money. Even though his wallet was full, his life was empty. Until, that is, Jesus showed up and gave him the second chance he needed.

> *Two words did it for Matthew. He didn't need a sermon or a miracle— just the calm, inviting tone of Jesus' words, "Follow me."*

Unfortunately, not everyone jumped for joy as high as Matthew did when he started following Jesus. Including a tax collector into the fold was a considerable shift for Jesus' group. Thus far, the people who followed Him were fishermen, farmers, women, and zealots. Each of them recognized their shortcomings and experienced long-suffering. Yes, they were sinners, but they could still lay their heads down at night and say, "God, I know I am a sinner, but at least I am not a tax collector."

It would be understandable if the disciples' reactions were, "Uh, Jesus, we sort of understand why You let the women come with us. You were stretching it when You invited the zealot. But now, tax collectors? Enough is enough. We have to draw the line somewhere." But before the jury of disciples could announce their unsolicited verdict on whether the tax-collecting traitor should be allowed into the fold, Matthew had already packed his sack, locked up his tax booth, and started following Jesus.

Matthew was ecstatic! He threw a party and wanted all his "tax collector and sinner" friends to share in his life change (v. 10). It just so happened that while Matthew was about to give a toast to Jesus, his honored guest, a few uninvited Pharisees were conveniently passing by Matthew's mansion and heard the commotion. To say they were appalled would be an understatement. Not necessarily because it looked like a tax collector convention, but because sitting in the middle of all these social outcasts was none other than Jesus Himself. The Pharisees thought that if Jesus was supposed to be some highly regarded rabbi, surely He would know that He was not supposed to mingle with such sketchy characters.

They asked Jesus' disciples, "Why does your teacher eat with tax collectors and sinners!" (v. 11). Scratching their heads, His disciples had no idea how to respond. They were as perplexed as the Pharisees but didn't have the Jewish *chutzpah* to ask Jesus. But before the disciples could even acknowledge the religious elites' question, Jesus interjected, "It is not the healthy who need a doctor, but the sick" (v. 12). Jesus left no doubt about His mission. The religious leaders thought the Messiah was coming to uphold the law. The political zealots thought the promised Messiah was coming to overthrow the Roman occupation. But Jesus clearly said He came for another reason: He came to give second chances to the least expected.

It is no surprise that in his account of the events, Matthew includes an extra bit of information that Jesus said that the other gospel writers left out. After all, tax collectors were detail-oriented people. Matthew wanted his primarily Jewish readers to remember one more thing Jesus said to the Pharisees: "But go and learn what this means." Then Jesus quotes a verse from the Old Testament: "I desire mercy, not sacrifice" (Matthew 9:13a; Hosea 6:6).

Those snobby scholars could have easily quoted any verse from the book of Hosea, let alone that particular one. But their head knowledge was not the issue. The problem was their lack of heart and compassion for those who needed a new beginning. Even though they were A+ students in making sacrifices to the Lord, they failed miserably at showing empathy and forgiveness to others. The very ones who were supposed to offer multiple chances to the outcasts were instead the ones who scoffed, sneered, and oppressed them. But Jesus made it clear: "I have not come to call the righteous, but sinners" (Matthew 9:13). The Pharisees found it unimaginable that God loves people like tax collectors and other sinners. But He does!

Matthew's story is a powerful reminder that Jesus welcomed everyone, no matter their past actions or mistakes. If one thing is clear about Jesus, He welcomed everyone to follow Him. He gave everyone a second chance. His message of forgiveness and redemption offers hope to all those in need of starting over. You may feel like the only ones who can move forward after messing up are those with more prestige or easier paths, but Jesus extends His hands and healing touch to everyone, including you.

Jesus seeks the unexpected and wants us to do the unexpected too.

It's hard to imagine that Jesus wanted a tax collector like Matthew in His circle, but He did. And it took a lot of courage for Matthew to leave his booth and follow Jesus. Jesus seeks the unexpected and wants us to do the unexpected too. No matter where you are in life, Jesus sees you as He saw Matthew and offers the same invitation, "Follow me." It's time to leave your past behind and start a new journey with Him.

RECOGNIZE THE CHANCES FOR NEW BEGINNINGS

Have you ever asked God for just one fresh start as a sign that He is present in your life? If you have, know that you are not alone. Many of us struggle with recognizing the new beginnings God has already given us. We focus so much on what we don't have that we fail to see the blessings right in front of us. The truth is that God gives us numerous small opportunities throughout our lives, but it's up to us to recognize them, take advantage of them, and use them as stepping stones to grow.

I'm sure that if we interviewed several people from the Bible, they would have said the same thing. But perhaps none would have been more adamant than Joseph from the Old Testament. His story is unique because unlike many others in the Bible, his hardships were mostly caused by others outside of his control. Imagine being betrayed by your own family and tossed into a deep, dark well to rot. That's how Joseph's second chance story started. But that was just the beginning. Despite being sold into slavery, separated from his family, and thrown into prison for a crime he didn't commit, Joseph held on to his faith in God. He understood that every moment, no matter how small, was a chance for God to reveal His perfect plan for Joseph's life.

Allow me to bring you up to speed on Joseph's story. Joseph had ten older brothers who were jealous of him. Together, they devised a wicked plan and threw him into an empty cistern. That would have been the end of his story, but Joseph continued to trust God. His brothers got another crazy idea and decided to sell him into slavery. A caravan dragged him hundreds of miles away, and he was bought off the slave block by a man named Potiphar. Still, the Lord continued to be with Joseph. Eventually, Joseph was put in charge of Potiphar's household because of his hard and honest work. Under those circumstances, things were as good as they could get. But then

Potiphar's wife developed an attraction to him, and he firmly resisted her advances. One day, she accused him of rape. Joseph was unjustly arrested, charged, and neglected in prison. It may have seemed like God abandoned Joseph, but He was working in the background. He was giving Joseph another chance.

After predicting a fellow inmate's future release, Joseph hoped his new prison friend would help set the record straight for him. After all, his new comrade was the Pharaoh's cupbearer. Surely this was a sign from the Lord. Now, Joseph's case would go directly to the feet of the most powerful person in the world, the Pharaoh of Egypt.

Every day, Joseph waited anxiously from his jail cell. He started daydreaming of walking on the beach at sunset and tasting fresh fruit from the market. But days turned to weeks, weeks to months, and months to years because "the chief cupbearer . . . did not remember Joseph; he forgot him" (Genesis 40:23).

It would have been hard for us to contain our frustration and anger. However, Joseph somehow continued to trust God during his times of loneliness. Somehow he realized that what others had meant for evil, God intended for good (Genesis 50:20).

In his darkest moments, Joseph never lost sight of God's promise to never leave or forsake him. He saw each twist and turn in his life as a stepping stone toward something greater. Even when betrayed, falsely accused, and forgotten, he kept his faith in God's goodness.

Joseph's journey was not without challenges. He could have easily given up on God and succumbed to bitterness and despair. But instead, he used each small moment as an opportunity to build his trust in God. Through it all, Joseph knew that God had a plan for him, and he was willing to wait for it.

Finally, after two years of waiting and hoping, Joseph's fresh start came. The cupbearer eventually remembered his fellow prisoner, and

Joseph was asked to interpret and predict Pharaoh's dream. Fast-forward a few showers, meals, and days later, and Joseph wins favor in the eyes of Pharaoh and receives something better than his freedom. Pharaoh appoints Joseph as second in command.[7]

Throughout his life, God repeatedly gave Joseph second chances. Some opportunities were more significant than others, but what remained the same was Joseph's trust in the Lord. How did he stay so hopeful in times of frustration and disappointment? Joseph could see all the small second chances in his life as stepping stones for his faith. One opportunity grew into another, and God used it for good.

In the end, Joseph's story shows us that God uses small moments as essential groundwork for our faith. Every moment of our lives, no matter how insignificant it may seem, is an opportunity for us to grow in our trust and confidence in God. Like Joseph, we can look back on our lives and see all the small fresh starts God has given us. We can use those moments to remind ourselves that God has a plan for us and is always working behind the scenes, even when we can't see it.

For a few moments: Similarly to Joseph, you may have been unjustly accused or harmed. Even though there may be times when it feels like God has abandoned you, He knows and sees your situation. He sees you. He has always seen you. He has been giving you new beginnings and small stepping stones all throughout your life.

For the next few moments, think about how God has specifically presented you with the chance of new beginnings throughout your lifetime, even in the smallest ways. For instance:

Has there been a time when you experienced a setback or failure (maybe you should have been fired from work or failed a class) but were given a chance to try again?

Were you ever in a romantic relationship that ended, but you can now see it was for the best?

Think about a time when you may have faced a difficult or painful experience but were able to find healing or growth as a result.

Are there any relationships in your life that have been restored or renewed after a period of distance or conflict?

Growing up, was there anybody in your life who brought you joy when you were in their presence? Maybe a grandparent, cousin, neighbor, or teacher? What would your life look like if you had never met them?

What small moments or details in your life has God orchestrated to bring you joy or provide a sense of peace and comfort?

By taking the time to reflect, you'll see that the God of Second Chances has been with you all along, even when it may not have felt like it. He has a way of revealing Himself in mysterious ways after the dust settles. So, if God was present in your life before, why doubt His presence now? If He could give you a new beginning in the past, He can give you a fresh start in the future. Remember how far He has already brought you and have faith that He has something greater in store for you. When you feel like there's no way forward, remember that He's not done with you yet.

LOOKING TO THE FUTURE

My brother Nick's journey to recovery continues to be far from easy. After being kicked out of his three-month rehabilitation center just days before completion, he found himself in a run-down motel on the outskirts of town, waiting for his trial. His future seemed bleak. Confined to his room because of his allergies to the harsh air quality conditions, he would only leave to walk to the grocery store, passing by the liquor store on the way. It was a difficult time, and there were moments when he called me, and I knew he was drunk, but I never stopped praying for him. Though the journey was slow and at times painful, he persevered, taking small steps forward until the day he stood before the judge, awaiting his verdict. With just a few words and a pen stroke, the judge's decision would dictate my brother's fate.

Having someone else prescribe our lives can be daunting. We want to be in control, calling the shots and charting our own course. When we relinquish our power, we are left feeling vulnerable. It is also challenging because choosing the path of least resistance is our nature. We want comfort, but sometimes what we need is discomfort. We want to keep the status quo, but we need to be challenged to mature. We seek freedom, but we need discipline. We desire fame, but we need humility. We often desire a life of leisure and wish to be in a place where our toes can sink into the warm sand and a refreshing drink is always at arm's length. However, what we truly need is a swift kick in the pants, tightly fastened boots, and a mindset ready to tackle any challenge that comes our way. Despite how tough it can be, in the end, what we very well may need to thrive and move forward after messing up is someone else speaking truth into our lives.

I'll tell you more of what my brother's judge told him in the next chapter, but for now, I want to talk to you more about you *and* the true and better Judge.

ENCOUNTERING THE TRUE AND BETTER JUDGE

Just as the judge had a plan and purpose for Nick's life, the true and better Judge, the God of Second Chances, also has a plan and purpose for your life. Thankfully, the true and better Judge is full of grace and truth. He doesn't merely preside in a courtroom, but rather He meets us where we are. He sees us beyond our mistakes and our sins. The God of Second Chances doesn't view us as society does. He doesn't even look at us the way we sometimes look at ourselves. He sees us as valuable, as worthy. And He has been using do-overs in our lives to get us closer to Him, one small step at a time. Don't believe me? Just ask the woman at the well in John 4.

Jesus was thirsty. After hours of walking, He and His friends had traveled miles. Their water pouches were as dry as the Judean desert. Their backs were tired, and their feet were sore. His friends barely had enough energy to go into town to purchase supplies. Jesus opted for staying on the outskirts of Samaria, near an old well. What seemed like a mere coincidence was actually a divine encounter. Jesus met a woman who needed to know that despite what the culture said about her, she had value in God's eyes and a second chance waiting for her.

She approached Him cautiously, not knowing who this strange man was. At first, there was silence, probably what she preferred. But then Jesus made a simple request, "Will you give me a drink?" (John 4:7). She quickly recognized by His complexion and accent that He wasn't from around those parts. Being a Samaritan, she also knew that it was not normal, sometimes even unacceptable, for Jews to associate with Samaritans.[8] So she was hesitant to respond to Jesus' request. Besides, this woman was way behind schedule. It was already midday.

She wanted nothing more than for the conversation to end so she could quickly leave. She had things to do and places to go. Collecting water was not something women would typically do under the hot noon sun. Instead, they would come to the well as a group in the mornings, so they had enough water for the day, and because there was safety in numbers. However, this woman came at noon. Did she oversleep? Was she running late? Probably not. Most scholars believe she went to the well alone at noon because she had been shunned by her friends, family, and the community. But why?

After a mostly casual conversation with the Samaritan woman, Jesus dove deep into her personal life. He suggested she ask her husband for help (v. 16). She replied, "I have no husband" (v. 17). Uttering those words and reliving the past in her mind must have been painful. She knew the truth about her past. What she didn't realize was that Jesus knew an even fuller version of that truth. Jesus reminded her that she had had five husbands, and the one she was with currently was not her husband (v. 18). Ah, there you have it. The reason she was at the well alone was that she lived a wild lifestyle and slept around. Or could there be another explanation for her loneliness and rejection?

It's easy to let the labels others put on you stick, but don't forget that God sees you for who you indeed are.

It is reasonable to assume that unfaithfulness kept her away from her friends. The common denominator in all of her relationships was her. But perhaps there is another reason she had been married so many times. Is it possible the common denominator goes deeper than just her choices? Perhaps the reason men tossed her aside and divorced her so frequently was not because of her infidelity, but rather because of her infertility.

If she had been unable to get pregnant, men would have quickly moved on from her. The women in her community would have looked down on her as inferior. She herself would have felt a personal shame. Society told her that she didn't matter and had no worth to them. Yet, when Jesus, the true and better Judge, encountered her at the well that hot afternoon, He saw her as precious and valuable. Jesus gave the woman another chance and an opportunity to gain eternal life from the only One who could provide it. Her new life began when she realized that all those marriages were second chances God used to bring her to this moment with Jesus.

This world can be harsh. People form half-baked views and cast judgment with ease. But instead of allowing them to label you as worthless, a junkie, a divorcée, troubled, or hopeless, remember that God sees you for exactly who you are, and you still matter to Him. You have always mattered to Him. It's easy to let the labels others put on you stick, but don't forget that God sees you for who you indeed are. He's been giving you new starts all along and wants to keep doing so.

Remember when you made a mistake or missed an opportunity, but things somehow worked out? Those were small stepping stones that were gifts from God. They were opportunities for you to grow, learn, and make things right. God's second chances are not reserved for the rich and famous or those with perfect lives. They are for everyone, everywhere. It doesn't matter who you are or where you come from, you are worthy of God's grace and mercy. You have the power to take control of your life and move forward with the second chances that God has given you.

So, if you're ready to accept the challenge, let's go, because we've got some work to do. It won't be easy, but it will be worth it. The road ahead may be rocky, but with God's guidance and grace, you can overcome any obstacle. Remember that every small step you take forward is another chance to grow and learn. And every time you stumble, remember that God is there to pick you up and give you stepping stones to a brighter future.

For Personal Reflection

1. Reflect on a time when you faced setbacks, failures, or difficult situations. How did you respond to those moments, and did they lead to growth, healing, or positive changes in your life?

2. How does the story of Joseph's life resonate with your own journey of overcoming your mess-ups? What lessons can you draw from his story about recognizing God's second chances and stepping stones in your life?

For Discussion:

1. Share a personal experience of a small second chance you received that helped you move forward. How can we actively recognize the second chances God has already given us in our lives, even in the smallest ways?

2. Think about the labels that others have placed on you or that even you have placed on yourself due to your past mistakes. How does knowing that God sees you as valuable and worthy challenge these negative perceptions?

3. Explore the story of the Samaritan woman at the well and how Jesus offered her a second chance. How can this story inspire us to approach others in need of a fresh start with compassion and understanding?

RISING THROUGH HUMILITY

Wisdom's instruction is to fear the LORD, and humility comes before honor.

PROVERBS 15:33

In a small town, two men attended the same church. One was a wealthy businessman who was highly respected in the community and known for his generous donations to the church. The other man was a struggling single father who had made some serious mistakes in the past. He was a janitor at a local school, and it was difficult for him to keep up with his monthly bills.

One Sunday at church, while the offering plate was being passed, the wealthy businessman got the pastor's attention and told the entire church that he was donating a check that would cover all the costs for the church's new building project. He looked at all of the smiling faces with a sense of satisfaction and felt a sense of pride for his contribution. Meanwhile, the janitor quietly placed a small amount of money into the basket and bowed his head in prayer.

After the service, the wealthy businessman greeted his friends and received compliments on his generosity. He looked at the janitor's life with criticism and thought, *How is it possible that a grown man is only able to have that job and give so little? If he was a real Christian, he wouldn't be in that situation.*

The janitor saw the look of shaming in the wealthy businessman's eyes, and he felt embarrassed. He knew he could not give as much as the businessman had. With a sincere and humble heart, he prayed silently, *God, forgive me for giving so little. Continue to have compassion on me and bless this man who thinks he is better than I am.*

What are your reactions when you read this story? Are you disgusted with the wealthy businessman? Do you feel empathy for the janitor? Are you shocked that, despite their differences, the janitor still prayed the way he did? I wonder if you would have felt the same way Jesus' listeners felt when He told a similar story found in Luke 18:9–14. In Jesus' account, the prideful Pharisee and the humble tax collector each went up to the temple to pray. The Pharisee proudly stood, front and center, for all to hear as he boasted about his abilities and actions. Whereas the tentative tax collector stood at a distance and begged God for mercy because he clearly recognized who he was in light of who God is.

RISE UP BY GETTING LOW

Jesus' story of the Pharisee and the tax collector captivated the group of people listening who were pleased with themselves over their moral performance and looked down at everyone else. In His story, instead of a wealthy businessman and janitor, Jesus' main characters were a self-righteous Pharisee and a humble tax collector. Jesus' point was that if you walk around with your nose in the air, you will end up flat on your face. But if you humble yourself, God will care for you and lift you up. Scripture teaches us, "God opposes the proud but shows favor to the humble" (James 4:6). In other words, you must get low before you can get up.

Your first step toward a second chance is humility. Of all the things to be in life, I think one of the hardest things to be is humble. Humility requires us to think outside of ourselves and consider others first. Someone has even quipped that humility isn't thinking less about yourself but thinking about yourself less.[9] The janitor in the opening story, and the tax collector in Jesus' story, were not perfect people. They had most likely made unwise decisions along the road. But they didn't let their situation dictate who they truly were on the inside. They had a proper perspective on life and God. They realized they had to humble themselves and get low before they could get up.

I can't think of many places that are more humbling than the courthouse. It is a place where people come to plead their case, but ultimately their fate is out of their hands. As I mentioned in the previous chapter, my brother Nick had to learn humility at the courthouse from the judge who oversaw his case. I'll tell you about the outcome later, but just knowing that someone else has the final authority to tell you where you will go and what you can and cannot do is a humbling feeling. It forces you to recognize the fact that "I am out of control. I need help. I need someone or something to help me control myself for my own good and the good of others." For Nick, it took standing before a judge for him to learn humility, but it doesn't have to be this way for everyone. We can learn humility from a lot of different places, but regardless of where we learn it, it is a lesson that must be learned.

THE CONNECTION BETWEEN HUMILITY AND MOVING FORWARD

Did you know humility is crucial to moving forward after messing up? The Spanish Augustinian friar Thomas of Villanova wrote, "Humility is the mother of many virtues because from it obedience, fear, reverence, patience, modesty, meekness and peace are born. He who is humble easily obeys everyone, fears to offend anyone, is at peace with everyone, and is kind with all."[10] Just like a solid foundation is essential to building a house, a strong footing of humility is vital for stepping into the second chance God has in store for you. While it would be wonderful to skip ahead to restored relationships with a renewed and energized future, some "behind-the-scenes" work needs to get done.

Not too long ago, my wife and I decided to get our bathroom re-modeled. The 1990s had called, and they wanted their style back. Since my hands do better on a computer keyboard than wielding a hammer, we hired a husband-and-wife team for our bathroom project.

Their small business was fantastic. In one day, they brought their trailer, dumpster, and group of several strong workers to demolish the entire bathroom. Based on the banging, you'd think they were playing a game of "Who can make the most noise while tearing out a bathroom?!" (and maybe they were), but when it was all said and done, the bathroom was completely gutted: studs exposed, traces of water damage visible, and electrical wires left dangling from the walls and ceiling. What took them half a morning would have taken me weeks, if not more. They were experienced at demolishing things and had all the right tools to make the job successful.

Now that the old was out, they had a blank slate. It still took several weeks to change the plumbing, retile, paint, do electrical work, and install the new vanity, tub, and toilet, but they got to start with a clean canvas. They had to do the dirty work first before they could begin rebuilding.

Out with the old and . . .

We must do some of the heaviest lifting on the front end when moving forward after messing up. We must get rid of the old before moving on with the new. It is crucial that we tear out the old walls of hate, bitterness, and ego and get down to the studs. Because at the studs of your life is where you will find humility, the foundation for moving forward.

Finding your "humility studs" will enable you to acknowledge your mistakes, take responsibility for your actions, and empower you to make positive changes. Again, you must get low before you can get up. When you are humble, you will be more open to learning from your past and creating a better future for yourself and those around you.

Have studs of humility to give you the strength and blank slate to start over and move forward.

If you are in the process of overcoming addiction, research shows that individuals who exhibited more humility were more likely to stay in treatment and less likely to relapse.[11] By admitting that they have a problem and seeking help, addicts can address the root causes of their addiction and learn new coping skills.

Another study found that humble individuals are more likely to see the value in repairing damaged relationships and are willing to take responsibility for their actions.[12] This willingness to apologize and make amends can lead to greater forgiveness and stronger relationships.

Maybe you want to grow as a person or leader in your family or career. Numerous studies have shown that being humble can have a positive impact on personal growth and leadership.[13] When we humble ourselves and get low, we are open to learning and improving ourselves, which can lead to greater success in our personal and professional lives. It also helps us connect with others and build stronger relationships, as humility makes us more empathetic and understanding toward others. By admitting our mistakes and being willing to learn from them, we can become better versions of ourselves and inspire others to do the same.

If you want to take the first step in taking your second chance, do some reflective thinking. Tear out the old walls of selfishness, pride, and self-centeredness. Realize that the world doesn't revolve around you, your situation, or your feelings. I'm not saying your condition and feelings aren't important—they are—but if that is what is primarily holding the walls of your life up, there is no wonder why you have, or will, come crashing down. Instead, get low so God can lift you up. Have studs of humility to give you the strength and blank slate to start over and move forward.

TRUE HUMILITY VS. FALSE HUMILITY

If we are going to learn to be humble, we must distinguish between true humility and false humility. In our culture of propaganda, misinformation, and falsehoods, it can be challenging to decipher through the multitude of images, stories, and actions people claim in the name of humility. So what, then, is true humility, and what does false humility look like?

I don't fly often, but I usually try to get a window seat when I do. Even though my legs are cramped, and it is hard to get in and out of my seat, I like the window seat because of the spectacular views. Looking out the window reminds me that life can be viewed from all different perspectives.

I especially enjoy looking out the airplane window during takeoff and landing. I try to identify landmarks and look for neighborhoods that are familiar to me. The skyscrapers of cities look like Legos. The cars on the interstate look like ants moving in all directions. Whenever I look out the airplane window, I am constantly reminded of how vast our world is, how small I am, and just how big God is. Looking at the world from above forces me to see myself and others in a whole new light. True humility is looking at the world from a different view, a heavenly perspective. Proper humility comes from seeing the world the way God sees the world.

But what does that mean, exactly? How do we do that? How do we look at the world from God's perspective every day? Several key characteristics of true humility are recognizing our limitations, practicing selflessness, looking at others with compassion, and expressing genuine gratitude while being willing to learn. Let's examine these aspects individually and see how they compare with what could be identified as "false humility."

RECOGNIZE YOUR LIMITATIONS

Recognizing that we have limitations is crucial to having true humility. Doing so allows us to clearly define reality instead of the lies we are told by the world and the lies we tell our- selves. Realizing our limits may, indeed, be the hardest part of having true humility. It is challenging to set aside our pride because it makes us seem weak and feels like we are putting a burden on others. But spotting our limitations helps us get back on our feet because it allows us to see something about ourselves that is hindering growth.

Once you identify the holes in your armor, you can get help to move forward and make yourself stronger than ever.

Admitting our limits can be difficult, but face it, if we are going to move forward after messing up, we have to know when to throw in the towel and acknowledge that we need help. When my wife, Ashley, was in college, she was a proud owner of a used 1998 Hyundai

Elantra. However, less than a year after she purchased it, the reverse decided to go on a permanent vacation. Not wanting to accept defeat and because she was a financially strapped college student, she refused to take it to the mechanic. So, for weeks, she had to be very strategic about how and where she parked. But since most parking spaces didn't allow her to pull all the way through, when she wanted to go somewhere, she would have to put "Old Faithful" in neutral, hang one foot out the door, and channel her inner Fred Flintstone. This strategy worked for a few weeks, but realizing that something needed to change, she worked overtime and saved up enough money to take her car to the mechanic to be fixed.

What are your limitations? Where do you need to ask for assistance? While you may think seeking help signals weakness, recognizing your limitations can become your greatest strength. Because once you identify the holes in your armor, you can get help to move forward and make yourself stronger than ever. Your greatest weakness may turn into one of your most vital attributes.

Lionel Messi, one of the greatest soccer players of all time, found a way to take his most significant weakness to make him an unstoppable force on the soccer pitch. Throughout his career, the renowned international superstar suffered from a well-documented performance anxiety. From the time he was a little boy, he often vomited either in the locker room or directly on the field during the game. It wasn't until midway through his career that he figured out a solution to overcome this setback. The answer was to take things literally one step at a time.

After the opening whistle, Messi would walk around slowly but purposefully instead of running after the ball. Even though it appeared he was not giving his total commitment and energy, he was actually calming his nerves. The other thing he was doing was surveying and studying his competition. By slowing down and observing his opponents, he learned about their formation, their weaknesses, and how he could expose the flaws in their game. He became an even better soccer player when he could recognize and accept his greatest weakness and limitation.

Limitations can be hard to acknowledge. They can even be embarrassing, like pushing your car in reverse or vomiting during a soccer game. Or more realistically for you, it's things like learning to live on a budget, being committed to exercising or eating a certain diet, or perhaps finding someone who can hold you accountable when you know you are tempted to fall. The reality is, when we face our weaknesses head-on, instead of pretending they aren't there, a tremendous number of possibilities open up for us to grow and succeed.

Practicing authentic selflessness

Another characteristic of true humility, as opposed to false humility, is practicing authentic selflessness. It is tempting to surrender your hands in defeat and wave the white flag of disappointment after another failed relationship or job rejection. Perhaps you are even tempted to post your circumstances on social media to get sympathy from others. But that is not a sign of true humility. That is simply thinking less of yourself and itching for attention. True humility is finding the art of practicing authentic selflessness.

Being genuinely humble demands us to put others' interests above our own and become "There-You-Are" people.

I've heard it said that there are two types of people in the world. No, I'm not talking about introverts and extroverts, dog lovers and cat lovers, or even Republicans and Democrats. I'm talking about

"Here-I-Am!" people and "There-You-Are" people.

"Here-I-Am!" people walk into a room and convey, *Here I am! Look at me! Let me tell you what is going on in my life, what I am doing, and what I am thinking.* But genuinely humble people are "There-You-Are" people. "There-You-Are" people walk into a room, look around, and express, "Ah, there you are! I've been wondering about you. How's the family? What's new with you? Were you ever able to get your motorcycle to work?" These people have a genuine interest in others. They aren't thinking less of themselves, but they are thinking of themselves less and putting others first.

When writing to a group of believers in the church located in Philippi, the apostle Paul encouraged them to become "There-You-Are" people. This is how he says it: "Do nothing out of selfish ambition or vain conceit. Rather, in humility value others above yourselves, not looking to your own interests but each of you to the interests of the others" (Philippians 2:3–4). Our nature is to be self-centered. But being genuinely humble demands us to put others' interests above our own and become "There-You-Are" people.

True compassion

Have you ever noticed how pleasant the names of subdivisions sound? I mean who wouldn't want to live in a place called Harmony Hills, Maplewood Gardens, or Sunrise Meadows? However, you and I both know that no matter what the name of the neighborhood is, neighbors don't always treat one another with true compassion. Sometimes our neighbors, coworkers, and even family members annoy us, avoid us, or just simply appall us. Regardless, God placed them in your life. But what does it mean to be a neighbor, and better yet, what does it mean to be a humble neighbor who shows compassion?

After a studious lawyer discussed eternal life with Jesus, he got a lesson in Neighboring 101 from the Master Himself. In one of the most well-known stories of the Bible, Jesus answers the question, "Who is my neighbor?" with a story. In His parable, Jesus describes the tragic scene of a man getting mugged on his way to Jericho. Two "leaders" in the community, people you would expect to help out, actually passed him by (Luke 10:31–32). The priest and the Levite both saw the man in need but, because of their religious practices, did not want to associate with or touch someone who seemed "unclean."

There would have been an audible gasp from Jesus' listeners as He continued the story and pronounced that it was actually a Samaritan who saw the man in need and had compassion for him (v. 33). The Samaritan's actions that followed were selfless, sympathetic, and sacrificial (vv. 34–35). This is why Jesus' listeners would have been stunned by his final question: "Which of these three do you think was a neighbor to the man who fell into the hands of robbers?" (v. 36). You can almost imagine the change in the lawyer's tone of voice when he gently answered, "The one who had mercy on him" (v. 37).

Jesus says we are to "go and do likewise" (v. 37). But what exactly are we supposed to do, and who precisely is our neighbor? It is pretty simple, actually; your neighbor is anyone who is in need, and you can help. Another word for this is compassion.

The word compassion comes from two Latin words that mean "suffering together." When you can say that you are suffering alongside someone because of their circumstances, you are beginning to practice true humility. But when you secretly root for someone else's failure or continually compare yourself to those around you, you are not being a humble and compassionate neighbor. On the other hand, when you begin to show true compassion for those whom you notice are in need, you take another step on the path of moving forward.

Genuine gratitude

"Don't forget to say 'thank you.'" If you are like me, your parents said this to you often when you were a child. And maybe you've given this advice to children yourself. But if we are honest with ourselves, even adults, and yes, even Christians, sometimes forget to express genuine gratitude and appreciation. Why do many of us struggle with remembering to give thanks or to show gratitude toward others? Why is it that giving thanks seems to slip our minds? Most of the time it is not because we aren't grateful, it's just because, often, giving thanks isn't as important as other things.

I struggle with this. I have forgotten to give thanks to people who have given me gifts. I have repeatedly failed to thank people who helped me with a favor. I am willing to guess you have too. But can you imagine forgetting to give thanks to, of all people, Jesus?

Jesus and His followers were on their way to Jerusalem for the last time to celebrate one of the Passover traditions (Luke 17:11). We don't know exactly which village Jesus entered, but we do know who was waiting for Him: a group with a horrible skin disease called leprosy (v. 12). By law, people with leprosy were forced to isolate, leaving their family, friends, and jobs, to live with others who suffered from a similar disease.

When Jesus passed, these suffering people recognized that this was possibly their one and only chance to get help. So together, they cried out to Jesus (v. 13). Jesus responded by telling them to see the priest who had the authority to allow them to rejoin society (v. 14). On their way to the local synagogue, they were miraculously healed! But then something even more remarkable took place. One man, the Samaritan—again, someone whom His followers would have least expected—paused and, before seeing the priest, turned back to Jesus to say, "Thank You" (v. 15).

Upon seeing him, Jesus asked, "Where are the other nine?" (v. 17). I'm sure all those in Jesus' presence who heard the question were perplexed. Were the others not grateful for their second chance too? Well, of course they were grateful. Each one of these people had experienced a life-altering miracle. But for one person, the Samaritan, he had a sense of genuine gratitude. So much so that his gratefulness for what Jesus had done turned into an outward expression of thankfulness. Being grateful is an emotion we feel, but having genuine gratitude is an action we can take.

We live in true humility when we genuinely express our gratitude toward others. Sometimes people will express false humility by giving lip service of thankfulness. They will too casually say "Thanks" because they know it is the right thing to say. But insincere gratefulness can be smelled from miles away.

True humility is when we turn our gratefulness into thankfulness. It's when we take time to pause out of our busy, hectic lives and express our gratitude. For some this may mean writing a thank-you note with words of appreciation; for others, it may be giving a thoughtful gift; for some, it may be offering a genuine and sincere handshake, smile, or hug.

Willingness to learn

In her book *Mindset*, Stanford professor Carol Dweck talks about the difference between having a fixed mindset and a growth mindset. She says that a fixed mindset is the belief that our abilities and intelligence are fixed traits that cannot be significantly changed. Her research found that those with a fixed mindset tend to avoid challenges, fear failure, and view effort as useless. On the other hand, a growth mindset is a belief that abilities and intelligence can be developed and improved through dedication, hard work, and perseverance.

Individuals with a growth mindset embrace challenges, see failure as an opportunity for learning, and understand that effort is crucial in achieving success. In other words, those with a growth mindset are eager to learn from their mistakes and grow.[14]

Dweck highlights the famous example of Thomas Edison's invention of the light bulb. Edison encountered numerous failures and setbacks while attempting to create a practical electric light bulb. Instead of viewing each failure as a definitive sign of messing up, he embraced a growth mindset. Edison famously remarked, "I have not failed. I've just found 10,000 ways that won't work." He approached each setback as an opportunity to learn and make progress.

In many ways, this is countercultural to our world today. Many well-known personalities and politicians believe that despite one's efforts, some people can never grow or thrive out of their circumstances. Undoubtedly, there are injustices in our societies, but Dweck advocates for a more optimistic outcome. Despite one's situation, she believes that when people are humble enough to learn from others and grow, there is very little that they cannot accomplish.

I had a history professor who would challenge us to learn by often saying, "As the island of knowledge increases, so do the shores of ignorance." I translated that as, "The more I learn, the more I realize I know very little . . . how exciting because there is so much more to discover!" For those with a fixed mindset, when their GPS stops working on their smartphone, they think disaster will ensue, but for those who have a growth mindset and willingness to learn, an adventure has just begun.

It takes true humility to have a growth mindset and a willingness to learn from others. But it is impossible to move forward unless we learn from those who have gone before us. God can't change the future of our lives and the lives of our loved ones unless we learn from our mess-ups and grow into the person that God ultimately wants us to be.

WHY PEOPLE STRUGGLE WITH HUMILITY

Just knowing the difference between true humility and false humility is not enough. We have to learn how to put humility into practice. The book of James says, "Who is wise and understanding among you? Let them show it by their good life, by deeds done in the humility that comes from wisdom" (3:13). However, the reality is that people struggle with being humble. You do, I do, we all do. Sometimes God has a way of teaching us how to be humble.

On June 11, 2021, off the coast of New England, lobster diver Michael Packard experienced something so rare it is hard to believe. He found himself inside the mouth of a humpback whale! "I was in his closed mouth for about 30 to 40 seconds before he rose to the surface and spit me out," he wrote on Facebook.[15] After his hospital release, Packard said that he hadn't expected to make it through the experience. Thankfully he lived, but talk about a way for the Lord to get someone's attention!

Jonah, from the eighth century BC, must have had similar thoughts as Packard when a great fish swallowed him after he refused to preach to the Ninevites. Jonah had one job: tell the Ninevites to repent because the Lord wanted them to know Him. But the problem was, Jonah hated the Ninevites! It's hard to blame him. They were idolatrous warriors with a reputation for cruelty. In other words, they had a lot to repent about. But Jonah's pride, fear, ego, and entitlement got in the way of his humility and the Ninevites' path toward God. So, before God could work in the lives of the Ninevites, He had to work on Jonah first. And if Jonah wouldn't humble himself, God would do the humbling for him in the form of a hurricane, a near-death drowning experience, and being swallowed by a giant beast of the sea.

While most people are familiar with the story of Jonah, we might overlook his prayer while he sank into the sea. The beginning of his prayer details the horrific experience of nearly drowning. The current swirled around him, the waves crashed overhead, and he started to drown (Jonah 2:3). As he continued to sink and seaweed wrapped around his head, he began to pray (vv. 5–7). Even from the depths of the sea, God still listened to his plea, and the Lord saved him from certain death (v. 7). Jonah's life is an example of an inconsistent walk with God and one's struggle with humility.

Let's face it, though, he's not the first or last person ever to struggle with humility. What gets in the way of your becoming completely humble? Perhaps it's your pride or self-image. Maybe you fear that something awful could happen if you give up control. For some, insecurity impedes one's ability to be humble. Maybe your ego or success got so big that it drowned out any possibility of being humble. Or perhaps greed or the quest for power caused you to focus on yourself and not others.

For Jonah, many things got in the way of his humility. He was supposed to be the one to rescue the pagan Ninevites from their idolatrous lifestyle, but it turns out there was a bit of Nineveh in Jonah. His pride and idolatry had taken over his life. But once Jonah humbled himself and prayed to God, a giant fish rescued him. Jonah later learned that a daily commitment to God meant being humble by putting aside vain idols. Jonah writes, "Those who cling to worthless idols, forfeit the grace that could be theirs" (Jonah 2:8). When we refuse to humble ourselves and cling to useless idols, we abandon any hope of mercy and grace.

Do you ever feel like you are drowning in a situation? No matter where you may be, God sees and hears you. Unfortunately, like Jonah, we often wait for times of desperation to cry to Him. What would you identify as reasons why you struggle with humility? What worthless idols are you clinging to? Don't lose out on what God wants to do in your life and the lives of those around you.

BEGINNING THE PROCESS TOWARD HUMILITY

Sometimes, if we don't humble ourselves, somebody else will humble us on our behalf. Jonah eventually realized that. I imagine you have realized that too. Perhaps your boss terminated your employment due to a series of repeated mistakes. Maybe your spouse gave you a full dose of reality by giving you an ultimatum to "Get clean" or "Get out." For my brother Nick, a judge gave him a sentence of grace and truth. Instead of penalizing him and sentencing him to serve time in prison, which would have been an appropriate consequence for his actions, he allowed him to enter a 90-day rehabilitation center. Throughout that experience, Nick learned the essence of true humility. While in rehab, he was able to recognize his weaknesses and limitations and was open to honest feedback from his peers and counselors.

What about you? What will be your process toward humility? Don't wait for someone else to humble you. Take the next steps toward humility now. You can start by recognizing your limitations, practicing selflessness, looking at others with compassion, and expressing genuine gratitude while being willing to learn. Begin practicing humility in small ways. Seek out others around you, strangers, or people you know, and be humble toward them. Allow one step of humility to lead to another, then another, and another. By taking it one step at a time, you will slowly cultivate a humble lifestyle.

I'm confident that when you take steps toward humility, you will begin to see the progress of moving forward that you, your loved one, and your heavenly Father have been desiring. But being humble is only one step toward moving forward, because close behind being humble is finding the ability to both extend forgiveness and seek it from others. If you want to truly move forward after messing up, then you have to learn the importance of forgiveness. So if you want to break free from the chains of the past and walk into a future unburdened by lingering feelings of anger or disappointment, then keep reading. Too much is at stake to stop now. Forgiveness holds the key to unlocking the life God wants for you.

For Personal Reflection

1. Think about a time when you experienced the consequences of pride or a lack of humility. How did that experience shape your perspective on the importance of humility in your journey of overcoming your challenges?

2. How has your past affected your ability to embrace humility and move forward? Are there any specific incidents or regrets that you struggle to let go of, and how might humility play a role in healing and growth?

For Discussion

1. Reflect on the characteristics of true humility, such as recognizing limitations, practicing selflessness, showing genuine

compassion, expressing gratitude, and being willing to learn. Which of these aspects do you find most challenging to embody, and why? Share examples from your life where you have experienced or witnessed these aspects of humility in action.

2. Discuss the reasons people might struggle with humility, as outlined in the chapter. Have you personally faced any of these challenges in embracing humility, and how have you dealt with them? How might your group members support each other in overcoming these obstacles?

3. How can you cultivate a growth mindset and a willingness to learn from your mistakes in your journey of recovery or personal growth? Share specific strategies or practices that have helped you—or will help you—adopt a more humble and open attitude toward your own growth and development.

6

FORGIVENESS IS THE KEY TO UNLOCKING YOUR FUTURE

Be kind and compassionate to one another, forgiving each other, just as in Christ God forgave you.
EPHESIANS 4:32

The most essential part of making pottery is your hands.

I learned this from my high school art teacher, who was teaching the class about pottery. She brought in molding clay for us to practice and experiment with over the course of a month. She taught us the significance of the clay, the wheel, and water. But I'll never forget what she emphasized: the key to creating something extravagant was controlling the movement and pressure of your hands.

One time, I was working diligently at the wheel, trying to carefully shape my lump of clay into a beautiful vase. However, I kept failing miserably. Either the clay continued slipping, or the wheel was spinning too fast, but regardless of the reason, the vase kept collapsing. I quickly realized that while I did have an Italian last name, I was no Michelangelo. My hopes and dreams changed from becoming a world-renowned artist to simply making it through the class with a passing grade and not throwing clay at my teacher. I continually had to smash the clay into a lump and start over again.

But imagine my teacher faced with this flawed creation. Someone who was much more experienced than me. This potter, too, could easily discard the creation, seeing it as a failed attempt. However, instead of giving up and returning the clay to its original ball-like form, the professional potter took a different approach.

An expert potter, like my teacher, could examine the blemished piece, study its imperfections, and realize that beauty can be brought out of the brokenness. This professional could begin to work with renewed determination, carefully reshaping and reforming the clay. The potter could add new layers, fill in the gaps, and mold the vessel into a new and unique design. Where all I could have managed to do was start over, the skilled potter sees something magnificent in the failure. As the work continues, the mistakes become part of the vase's story, contributing to its character and beauty. Ultimately, what was once a flawed and broken piece of clay transforms into a stunning work of art.

GOD AND DAMAGED CLAY

Just as the skilled potter doesn't give up on damaged clay, God does not reject us when we mess up. Instead, He sees the brokenness and imperfections and lovingly works to reshape us into something beautiful. This is called the power of redemption, and it begins with forgiveness.

God's forgiveness is like the potter's hands, gently and skillfully reshaping our lives. He doesn't discard us as unworthy or irreparable. Instead, He uses our brokenness to create a unique story of redemption and transformation. He takes our ordinary mess and turns it into an extraordinary message. We can find healing, restoration, and a renewed sense of purpose through His grace and forgiveness.

Remember that no matter how much you may have messed up or how deeply broken you feel, God's love and forgiveness are always available. He is the master artist who can transform our brokenness into something beautiful. Sadly, though, even though the Master Potter has hands of grace and forgiveness, we still struggle with allowing Him to shape us into the person He wants us to be.

THE KEY IS IN YOUR HAND

In John Bunyan's timeless masterpiece, *The Pilgrim's Progress*, the protagonist Christian embarks on a journey to the Celestial City. Along the way, he encounters various obstacles and distractions that hinder his progress. Particularly challenging is the burden he carries at the start of his pilgrimage, symbolized by an oversized, weighty pack. As Christian reflects, "I was burdened with a great load, a weight that I had carried my whole life."[16] His burden nearly kills him by sinking in the Swamp of Despair as well as causing him several times to question his long, treacherous journey toward a new life.

If you could use a key to unlock your future and be freed from the weight of your burden, would you use it?

However, at the Place of Deliverance, as Christian wearily approaches the crest of a hill, he spots a towering wooden cross. Drawing nearer, he feels the straps on his shoulders suddenly snap and the tremendous load he had carried all his life tumble off his back. At that moment, he experiences true liberation. He is finally free. He can now embrace a life of liberty and boundless joy. Christian's burden had been forgiven because he gave it all over to God at the cross.

What burden have you been carrying that has caused you to stumble? The author of Hebrews says that our sin can easily entangle us from living the life God wants for us (Hebrews 12:1–3), but forgiveness is the key to unlocking our future's potential.

Unfortunately, not everyone is ready to ask Jesus to remove their burden and give it to God. What about you? If you could use a key to unlock your future and be freed from the weight of your burden, would you use it? If you are not ready yet, that is okay. But I will be upfront with you: throughout this book, I have alluded to surrendering your life to the Lord, and at the end of this chapter, I am going to ask you to take the key of forgiveness out of your pocket and unlock the door that leads to the future God wants for you. One of your hesitations may be thinking that the God of Second Chances could never forgive you. If that is the case, you are not alone.

GOD OFFERS FORGIVENESS TO EVERYONE . . . EVEN YOU

There are a lot of misconceptions when it comes to forgiveness. For instance, some believe the lie that forgiveness is about denying or overlooking the hurt and pain actions cause. In reality, true forgiveness is feeling the hurt and releasing it to God. Forgiveness doesn't mean explaining away the hurt; it works through the hurt. But probably the biggest misconception about forgiveness is the notion that it cannot be extended to everyone, especially you.

In the film *The Avengers*, the antagonist, Loki, attempts to manipulate and challenge Natasha Romanoff, also known as Black Widow, by reminding her of her past actions as a Russian spy.[17] In her quest to rescue her friend Clint Barton, Loki questions why she would want to save someone like Barton. Romanoff, haunted by her past mistakes, believes that saving her friend will bring her peace. In response to Loki's taunts, she refers to her past lifestyle as a Russian assassin and states, "It's really not that complicated. I got red in my ledger. I'd like to wipe it out."

The conversation dynamics change when Loki counters with a series of harsh accusations. He questions whether Romanoff can genuinely erase the extent of her dark deeds. "Can you? Can you wipe out that much red?" Loki says. "Dreykov's daughter, São Paulo, the hospital fire? Barton told me everything. Your ledger is dripping. It's gushing red, and you think saving a man no more virtuous than yourself will change anything? This is the basest sentimentality. This is a child at prayer, pathetic! You lie and kill in the service of liars and killers. You pretend to be separate, to have your own code. Something that makes up for the horrors. But they are part of you, and they will never go away." Loki is accurate in recounting Romanoff's past. She did those horrible deeds. Her ledger was dripping with red.

The truth is, we have red in our ledger too. It may not be red with murder, but we have killed opportunities and relationships. When you pause long enough to examine your past accurately, you realize that you have deeply hurt others and would do anything to correct those wrongs. But once we have sinned against God or others, that sin becomes an inseparable part of us. As Loki said, "They are part of you, and they will never go away." We become sinners, and it seems as though the stain of those transgressions can never be removed or washed away.

The beauty of the gospel presents a different outcome. The apostle Paul writes,

> If anyone is in Christ, the new creation has come: The old
> has gone, the new is here! . . . God made him who had no sin

to be sin for us, so that in him we might become the righteousness of God. (2 Corinthians 5:17, 21)

Through Christ's sacrificial work on the cross, He died the death we should have died, and He cleansed our ledgers with His perfect life. As a result, if we have received forgiveness from God, He no longer sees any red in our ledger. Instead, our sins have been placed upon Christ, and His righteousness has been transferred and accredited to us. When God looks at us, He sees the perfection and purity of Christ. That is the essence of forgiveness.

A SERIOUS SINNER REPENTS

There are some awful characters throughout Scripture, but you will be hard-pressed to find anyone more evil than King Manasseh. In 2 Chronicles 33:1–9, we read of the wretchedness and carnage performed at the hands of this detestable king. In these few verses, we learn that King Manasseh:

desecrated Solomon's temple with idols,
worshiped pagan gods,
murdered his own children as a sacrifice,
led people astray.

Clearly, this man was pure evil (vv. 2, 6, 9). Though the Lord spoke to him, he continually turned a deaf ear (v. 10). He arguably did more to encourage idolatry, which eventually led to the Babylonian invasion and captivity of the Jewish people, than any other king throughout history. Eventually, he was captured by the Assyrians, a brutal and humiliating occurrence for this king of Judah (v. 11).

Yet even though Manasseh was a horridly evil person, God loved him and gave him another chance. In an astounding turnabout, Manasseh humbled himself, sought God, and asked for forgiveness. Through prayer, he confessed his sin (v. 19) and acknowledged that Yahweh was God (v. 13). His genuine repentance was evident because when the Lord helped him return to Jerusalem, he changed his life and leadership. He made it clear to all that idolatry was an abomination, and he would worship Yahweh as God (vv. 15–17).

The short chronicle of Manasseh's life was included in Scripture, so future generations would know how to recover from the sin that led to their captivity. How far does God need to go to get your attention? Only humility and repentance stand between you and God's forgiveness. But not only do we need to rewrite our relationship with God, but we also need to incorporate forgiveness with those around us.

RECEIVE AND GIVE FORGIVENESS

Judge Frank Caprio has hundreds of millions of views of his courtroom verdicts on social media. But it is not his harsh words to criminals that attract viewers, it is the ways he reveals his compassionate heart. The eighty-year-old judge attempts to see the person behind the crime with every verdict. He realizes that his job is to deliver both grace and truth. However, this task is never easy. But as Scripture teaches us, Jesus came both full of grace and truth (John 1:14) so we can look to Him as our model.

For instance, one time, after Jesus was finished teaching on church discipline, Peter inquired what to do regarding lesser offenses that require forgiveness. In typical Peter fashion, he asked a question in a way that implied he already knew the answer, "Lord, how many times shall I forgive my brother or sister who sins against me? Up to seven times?" (Matthew 18:21). Peter's suggestion of seven is significant. Typically, Jewish rabbis taught people that they should forgive others three times. Perhaps trying to impress Jesus, Peter suggested forgiveness ought to be given seven times, the perfect number in Jewish tradition. But Jesus doesn't beat around the bush and answered, "I tell you, not seven times, but seventy-seven times" (v. 22). Jesus' response of "seventy-seven times" indicated there should be no restrictions on the number of times we forgive.

Jesus followed His formal answer to Peter with a story highlighting the generous forgiveness of a king who forgave his servant. Even though the servant owed his master an immense amount of money, the master forgave him. But the twist of Jesus' parable was that the same servant could not forgive another fellow servant who only owed him a few bucks. Even though the servant was forgiven by his master king for an extraordinary amount of money, he would not extend forgiveness to his fellow servant, who owed him a few coins. Though the servant had been given a second chance, when he had the power to give someone else a second chance, he refused (vv. 23–35).

If we cannot forgive others who have failed or betrayed us, then we don't truly realize how much we have been forgiven. Grasping how much we have sinned against God and His forgiveness toward us challenges us to give others a second chance too. The apostle Paul writes, "Be kind and compassionate to one another, forgiving each other, just as in Christ God forgave you" (Ephesians 4:32).

One day out of the blue, "Jeff" called me. He couldn't find "Amanda," his wife. He had tried to reach her again and again by phone but to no avail. I went over to his house to see if I could help in any way, and when I got there, he filled me in on what was really going on. His wife was having an affair.

Jeff admitted he was not completely shocked when he learned

about this. He had sensed something was brewing. The sneaking around, the hiding of text messages, and Amanda's vague responses to ordinary questions were indicators to him that his wife was no longer invested in their relationship and that the marriage was falling apart.

Jeff also shared that he was partially to blame. Though he hadn't been unfaithful with another woman, his work had consumed his life, and his marriage had become low on his list of priorities. Looking back, he had to admit that there had been too many times of his just not being available to Amanda and their children, both now grown. Too many events that didn't include her. Too little real conversation. Too many dismissals of her needs.

After hours of no contact that day, he finally got hold of Amanda. She wasn't physically too far away but had rented an apartment in the next town. She insisted that her relationship with the other man was meaningless and not permanent, and the real reason she had an affair was because of her anger with Jeff. Several days later, she agreed to meet Jeff at a restaurant to talk. He hoped they could possibly try to salvage their marriage. But their relationship would never be the same. Though they both tried individual counseling and even counseling as a couple, the marriage, at least in Amanda's eyes, was too far gone to be restored. They decided to get a divorce. Jeff, especially, was heartbroken.

After the papers were signed and the divorce was finalized, I still met with Jeff regularly. And even though his wife's affair was the worst thing anyone had ever done to him, I was impressed that he was able, with time and counsel, to truly forgive Amanda, admit his own faults, and forgive himself too.

Whom do you need to forgive? While this person may never come to you asking for forgiveness, that does not mean you cannot extend forgiveness to them. Forgiveness is not about forgetting what happened in the past. It is necessary to remember the past before we can forgive. Just like we must remember our past and how much God has forgiven us. And if we have been forgiven much, we must also forgive much.

FORGIVING THE PERSON IN THE MIRROR

I don't know about you, but I am moved by stories of forgiveness. I wish I could have the same power and courage to forgive as some others do. I've witnessed friends and family members who have embraced forgiveness and reconciled with one another, even after enduring hurt and wrongdoing. I have seen churches extend forgiveness to their pastors, even in the face of inappropriate misconduct. I'm especially moved when I see in the news that family members of a victim find it in their hearts to forgive the person responsible for their loved one's murder. These powerful examples of forgiveness embody extraordinary acts of courage and grace.

Yet, amid all these instances of forgiveness, the one person people have the most difficult time forgiving is the person they see daily in the mirror. Forgiving ourselves can be a monumental challenge, and it is crucial to understand why. Several reasons contribute to this internal struggle.

One reason we find it difficult to forgive ourselves is that we often hold the standards for ourselves higher than we do for others. The expectations we set for ourselves are near perfection. So, when we fall short of these self-imposed ideals, we struggle mightily to accept our brokenness and shortcomings. It's hard to forgive ourselves when we continuously fail to meet the impossibly high bar we've set for ourselves. Don't get me wrong, I think we should have high standards for ourselves and work hard to live lives that are meaningful and worthy of respect and honor. However, we often place the threshold of righteous living beyond what is realistically attainable.

Another reason forgiving ourselves can be challenging is the weight of guilt and shame that burdens our conscience. When we realize how our mess-ups have impacted those around us, the task of forgiveness becomes overwhelming. This is especially true when our actions affect our children or other loved ones. The more we care about someone, the more excruciating it feels to acknowledge our mess-ups, thus rendering self-forgiveness an incredibly challenging task. Sometimes people feel unworthy of forgiveness or feel they must continue to punish themselves for the pain and heartache they have caused their loved ones.

For some, the struggle to forgive themselves arises from the false idea of allowing our past to define us. We internalize our former actions to such an extent that they shape our self-image and self-worth. Instead of seeing ourselves as valuable beings created by God, we view ourselves solely through the lens of our past mistakes.

Last, fear plays a significant role in our reluctance to forgive ourselves. The fear of allowing the past to repeat itself can erect barriers to self-forgiveness. In the next chapter, we will delve into these fears, particularly the fear of relapse and of making future mistakes. But there is no doubt that many struggle with forgiving themselves because they don't trust themselves to make wise decisions moving forward.

ASKING GOD FOR FORGIVENESS

I've heard it said, "Forgiveness is for giving *it* over to God." What do you need to give over to God? What do you need to release from your grip? It is different for each of us. For instance, it may be the resentment we hold against someone who wronged us, the guilt we feel for our own shortcomings, or the grudges we harbor toward others. It could be the hurtful words that still echo in our minds, the bitterness that lingers from past disappointments, or the weight of unhealed wounds. Each person's "it" is unique and deeply personal. Still, the path to forgiveness begins by acknowledging and confronting these burdens and ultimately choosing to give "it" to God and find healing from Him.

Nick eventually realized that others had been victims of his addiction. Through some deep soul-searching and reflection, he came to the conclusion that his drug and alcohol addictions had been wrecking not only his life but the lives of those around him. It had been years since he had spoken to most people in our family, especially our mom. But while in rehab, he found the courage and strength to ask for forgiveness and penned this beautiful and compassionate letter to her asking for forgiveness:

Mom,

I hope this finds you well and that it won't be hard on you to read. I've realized in the past few months that you have been a victim of my addiction. For the last several years, my addiction has been the root of many of the ways I thought and things I believed. Most importantly I have not been honest with myself, and if I couldn't be honest with myself, it was impossible to be honest with you. Because of my lack of truth, I also don't remember or even realize the many ways I have been dishonest with you.

But I think the more hurtful fact is that I stopped communicating with you because I blamed you and thought I was the victim. I selfishly blamed you for the reasons I behaved badly. For excuses as to why I wasn't living up to my potential and choosing to live the life I was living. Being homeless made it easier for me to blame others and for my resentment to grow. I wrongly believed I deserved things I never earned. I lost things I didn't take care of. However, now that I have lost everything, including my dog, whom I love, I realize how hard it is to lose someone you love. Because you were never taken from me, I didn't understand I lost you. I also didn't see how my addiction took me away from you. Not only have I chosen to allow my thinking to disguise the loss, I used it to blame others for it. I'm now beginning to understand I am not the only victim of my addiction. I am also not the only one which was hurt the most by it.

I'm sorry I let drinking come between us and gave alcohol more love than you. I'm sorry for blaming you for my behavior. I'm sorry for not understanding how alcohol took me away from you. I'm sorry for not realizing that you are a victim of my addiction. I only hope now I can be honest with myself and you. I hope more that losing my addictive thinking will stop causing you to be a victim of my behavior.

Love,
Nick

This is what true repentance looks like. True and lasting healing begins when you can honestly identify your failing and give "it" over. Forgiveness is the only path that can lead to true reconciliation. Thankfully for Nick, my mom, and our family, reconciliation has begun. Not long after she received this letter, she and her sisters traveled across the country to visit him. It is impossible to move forward after messing up without asking for and extending forgiveness.

RESTORING YOUR RELATIONSHIP
WITH THE HEAVENLY FATHER

What if I were to tell you that an even more profound and restored relationship is within your grasp? It is the relationship that requires restoration between you and your heavenly Father. The journey toward this healing begins when we acknowledge and repent of our sins. I understand that the terms "repent" and "sins" are deeply rooted in religious language, and we don't frequently use them in our everyday conversations. However, these words accurately convey the essence of seeking and receiving forgiveness. At its core, the term "repent" means to change one's thinking, and the word "sins" means anything contrary to God. In other words, to repent of sins means to make a 180-degree turn in life because of a sincere desire to change for God and the good of others.

Christians don't do good deeds to be forgiven, but rather they do good deeds because they are forgiven.

So when you are ready to restore your relationship with the God of the universe, simply confess with your mouth that you are indeed a sinner and have been living contrary to Him and His ways. Either out loud or in the quietness of your heart, acknowledge that Jesus' death on the cross was so your sins could no longer be counted against you. And that Jesus was raised from the dead, confirming that He has the power and authority to forgive your sin. Here is a sample prayer. You can pray these exact words or use your own words. Either way, God will know your sincerity and accept you as His child:

"God, I repent of my sin. Jesus' death and resurrection made it possible for me to have a relationship with You. So, through the power of the Holy Spirit, I surrender my life to You and make Jesus my Lord and Savior."

And it's important to know that the truth of Jesus' death and resurrection—as well as what we do to make these truths personal—are all rooted in Scripture, God's Word to us.[18]

Many people believe that they are forgiven if they do enough good deeds. But this thinking is backward. Christians don't do good deeds to *be* forgiven, but rather they do good deeds because they *are* forgiven. As you begin to realize more and more what God has done for you through the sacrifice of Jesus, you can't help but want to change how you live.

That's it. That is all it takes to ask for forgiveness. A confession to God for the sin in your life and the trust that Jesus takes away our sins through His death and resurrection. There is no holy person you need to speak with; you can talk directly to God Himself because He is always listening. There is no particular place you need to travel to; simply dwell in His presence and surrender your life to Him. There is no book you need to finish reading or class you need to take; simply allow Him to write the narrative of your life and complete the race He wants you to run. It all begins with that initial conversation with Him, identifying your sin and giving "it" over to Him. So, let me ask you, are you ready to ask and receive forgiveness from Him?

Forgiveness is simple but at the same time hard. It takes both humility and sacrifice. But to truly move forward after messing up and to have restored relationships it is unquestionably necessary, and it is absolutely worth it! There is nothing that compares to the transformative power of extending forgiveness to others and receiving it in return. There is a tremendous amount of peace that comes through forgiveness. A peace like you have never experienced before awaits you when you surrender your life to the God of Second Chances. He is eagerly awaiting to remove your burden. Through His work on the cross, He has already taken care of the payment and punishment for your sins—all you have to do is receive His forgiveness and extend it to others.

Personal Reflection:

1. In what ways have you struggled to forgive yourself for past mistakes and shortcomings? How have these struggles affected your journey to move forward?

2. In what ways can you identify with Nick of seeking forgiveness from loved ones? How might his journey inspire you to seek forgiveness and reconciliation in your own life?

Group Discussion:

1. Share a personal experience of forgiveness that has had a significant impact on your life. How did that act of forgiveness transform your relationships and perspective?

2. Discuss the challenges and barriers individuals face when seeking to forgive themselves.

3. How does the concept of "giving it over" to God and others resonate with you? How can this principle be practically applied in your daily life to promote forgiveness and healing?

7

"DADDY, I KEEP FALLING!"

The LORD makes firm the steps of the one who delights in him; though he may stumble, he will not fall, for the Lord upholds him with his hand.

PSALM 37:23–24

She squealed like a hyperactive elf on a candy cane sugar high running through Santa's workshop.

When our daughter Adeline was four, she unwrapped her pink princess bicycle with training wheels on that chilly Christmas morning, and we knew she had a world of adventure waiting for her. Though the frosty December air prevented her from riding right away, she eagerly anticipated the day when she could pedal freely in the warmth of the sun. And when that first hint of spring arrived, she wasted no time. With determination in her eyes, she asked if she could take her bike for a spin in the driveway.

Watching Adeline struggle to hop on and muster the leg strength to push those pedals down, I couldn't help but feel a sense of responsibility as her dad. I stood behind her, gently pushing her up the small incline, grateful for the steadying presence of the training wheels that gave her a fighting chance.

The next summer, Adeline became determined to shed those training wheels and ride like the older girls in the neighborhood. I removed the wheels and assisted her in mounting her two-speed. I thought, *She's got this. By the end of the day, or at least the week, she will be zipping down the street enjoying the freedom of the fresh summer air like I did when I was a kid.*

Reality had a different plan. Adeline struggled—a lot. Without training wheels, she was continuously wobbling and veering off course. I tried to help as best I could. Holding on to the back of her seat proved ineffective as she fought to steer straight. Attempting to grip both the seat and the handlebar while also running alongside her only led to an awkward scene. Each time I let go, she would inevitably topple over, sometimes catching herself but often colliding with curbs or bushes. Frustration etched on her face. She looked up at me, tears welling in her eyes, and uttered those heartfelt words, "Daddy, I keep falling!"

GET UP AND DUST YOURSELF OFF

Throughout that summer, we dedicated ourselves to teaching Adeline how to ride without the training wheels, but to no avail. Despite her determined efforts and our help, she kept falling, but she refused to give up. Trying again and again, even in the face of countless failures. As autumn approached and winter settled in, her pink princess bicycle found its place in the garage, stored away for another season. At times, I tried to put the blame elsewhere. I thought, *Maybe it is the bike's fault. Perhaps it is simply too big for her.* But truthfully, as a father, I felt like I failed her.

The following spring arrived, and I braced myself for another round of bike-riding challenges. But to my astonishment, before I even had the chance to suggest it, I glanced out to the driveway and saw our now six-year-old Adeline riding her bicycle all by herself. A surge of pride washed over me as I marveled at my child's seemingly newfound abilities. Did she wake up that morning with a sudden burst of biking prowess she hadn't possessed the summer before? Perhaps, but most likely, no. What propelled her was the resilience she had cultivated from the previous summers. Despite the countless falls, she refused to surrender.

Time and time again, she would pick herself up, dust off her knees, take breaks when needed, but then leap back onto that bike. The word for that is resilience. In fact, the word "resilience" finds its roots in a Latin word that means "to rebound" or "to leap back."[19] It embodies the notion of encountering setbacks or failures yet finding the strength and support to rise again. Resilience reflects the capacity of an individual to overcome adversity, learn from their mistakes, and persevere in the face of challenges. But being resilient is not just reserved for little girls trying to learn how to ride a bike without training wheels. Being resilient is a virtue that anyone can possess. And I think the people who need it the most are those who keep falling. People like you and me.

So, what happens when you are given a second chance at life, when signs of progress emerge, and you are just starting to get back on your feet, only to be followed by a stumble that sends you flat on your face again? In this chapter, we will explore the issues that contribute to our minor slipups or full-blown relapses. We will delve into the art of identifying our specific triggers and equipping ourselves to sidestep potential pitfalls. In addition, I will encourage you to participate in a few exercises along the way. But before we learn how to rebound and ride once more, we must first become intimately acquainted with our heavenly Father, who is everpresent, ready to extend His helping hand and lift us up when we need Him most.

HE REALLY IS "GOD, *THE FATHER*"

You may have heard this before, but the term "gospel" means "good news." The good news for us is that when we stumble and fall, we have a heavenly Father there to lift us up. In fact, did you know that the way Jesus wants us to address the God of Second Chances is "Father"?

In the Old Testament, the title "Father" was used sparingly, mainly when the entire nation of Israel cried out to God. However, in the New Testament, Jesus had a special affection for referring to God as "Father." In fact, He used this name over 275 times in the Gospels. When His disciples asked Him to teach them how to pray, Jesus replied, "When you pray, say, 'Father, hallowed be your name'" (Luke 11:2). But not just any father, but specifically *Abba*, which could be translated as "Dad."

Jesus wanted His disciples, and us, to know that when we pray, we can approach God just as a child would call out to his or her loving father, saying, "Dad!" This sets Christianity apart from any other religion. In other faiths, God is often addressed as Supreme Being, Master, or One and Only God. For deists, it's Divine Providence. In the twelve steps of Alcoholics Anonymous, the term Higher Power is used. But when the disciples asked Jesus how they should address God, He tells them, call Him your heavenly Dad.

Have you ever considered how involved your heavenly Dad is with you? Renowned Christian author Max Lucado beautifully captures this truth when he writes,

> If God had a refrigerator, your picture would be on it. If he had a wallet, your photo would be in it. He sends you flowers every spring and a sunrise every morning. Whenever you want to talk, he'll listen. He can live anywhere in the universe, and he

chose your heart. And the Christmas gift he sent you in Bethlehem? Face it, friend. He's crazy about you.[20]

No one loves you more than your heavenly Father does.

I can't think of a greater picture of this in the Scriptures than when Jesus told a story about two sons and a father. The younger son essentially told his father that he wished he would hurry up and die so he could receive his inheritance. The son then went off and squandered his inheritance on worldly pleasures and eventually hit rock bottom. However, when the younger son finally came to his senses and decided to return home, what did his father do? His dad spotted him from afar and ran to him with open arms. He embraced him, showered him with kisses, and celebrated his return by clothing him in the finest robe, adorning him with a signet ring, and throwing a great feast. (You can read about this in Luke 15:11–24.) That's the depth of love your heavenly Father has for you, even after you fall.

So, my friend, it's time to face it and embrace it: God's love for us—for you—is deeper than we can even fathom. That's why Jesus encourages us to talk to Him, pour out our hearts, and share our deepest desires and struggles. So, when you stumble or find yourself falling repeatedly, Jesus says to call out to Him, and when you do, call Him "Dad." Now that we know how to address God after we fall, what are we supposed to do next?

DELILAH'S HOLD ON SAMSON

In the ancient times of Israel, one man stood out among all others for his unmatched strength: Samson. His story is a captivating yet cautionary tale that holds valuable lessons as we navigate the treacherous minefields that can lead to our downfall. Though he was gifted with extraordinary strength by God, Samson's weakness for love and recognition became his undoing.

Samson was sought after by women and envied by men. But his path took a treacherous turn when he fell for a captivating and cunning woman named Delilah, as recounted in Judges 16. Unbeknownst to Samson, Delilah was an instrument in the hands of the Philistine army, seeking to unravel the secret behind his extraordinary strength. Delilah repeatedly tested Samson's loyalty, yet her efforts proved futile.

Despite these unsuccessful attempts, Samson failed to fully grasp the gravity of the situation. He continued his relationship with Delilah without establishing essential boundaries. Delilah persisted in her deceptive pursuits, aiming to uncover the truth about his unmatched strength.

Unfortunately, Samson did not recognize what was truly going on. He remained blind to the potential risks he faced. Eventually, she discovered the secret to his strength was his commitment to the Nazarite vow. Part of the vow was to never cut his hair, but while he was asleep one night, she secretly pulled out the scissors and snipped off those luscious locks.

It wasn't his hair that gave him strength, but God gave him the power he needed as long as Samson kept the vow. Sadly, Samson could not discern that Delilah was not someone he ought to associate with, and after she exploited him, he was bound and imprisoned and practically sentenced to death. Samson failed to learn from his experiences and to recognize the high-risk situation he had put himself in by associating with Delilah.

IDENTIFY YOUR DELILAH

Now, consider this: Who, what, or where is your Delilah? What person, thing, or place seems to have a hold on you? Deep down, you know that whenever you are in its presence, you feel an undeniable urge to give in to temptation. You might find yourself justifying its importance and necessity in your life, even though you recognize its negative influence. Whatever, whomever, wherever it may be, it is crucial to acknowledge that this trigger acts as your personal Delilah.

Identifying your Delilah is essential to personal growth and overcoming destructive patterns. It requires honest introspection and a willingness to confront the uncomfortable truth about this trigger's impact on your well-being. Your Delilah could take the form of a substance, a behavior, a toxic relationship, a specific location, or any other form of temptation that exerts power over you. Recognizing your Delilah allows you to gain insight into the underlying reasons behind its hold on you. It may stem from emotional vulnerabilities, past traumas, or a need for validation and acceptance. Understanding these dynamics empowers you to develop strategies to navigate the challenges it presents and provides a way forward to break free.

Acknowledging your triggers is not a sign of weakness but rather a display of self-awareness and strength. It empowers you to take control of your choices and make conscious decisions that align with your values and long-term overall health.

Remember, identifying your Delilah is a personal journey that requires courage, self-reflection, and vulnerability. I would encourage you to seek support from trusted friends, mentors and pastors, or professionals who can provide guidance and encouragement along the way. By facing your triggers head-on, you can create a plan and implement healthy coping mechanisms to regain control of your life and chart a course that God wants for your future.

RECOGNIZING RED FLAGS

Year after year, drownings occur on the beaches around the country, often because swimmers fail to adhere to the warnings conveyed by the red flag. Red flags flying high indicate that the water is far too dangerous for swimmers. The cause of most drownings is usually a result of the deadly undertows that are difficult to see from above the water's surface. Undertows are underwater currents that pull the water from the shore out into the ocean. When swimmers are caught in an undertow while their head remains above water, they often try to swim back to shore. Unfortunately, trying to swim against the ocean's underwater current is like swimming upstream in a river. Swimmers usually panic, exhaust themselves, and then sadly drown. Despite the red flags hoisted by lifeguards and city officials, swimmers miss or disregard the clear warning signs, leading to far too many tragic incidents. The reality is, if swimmers recognize and follow the warning signs of the beach's red flags, there would be a lot more future vacations with loved ones.

If you are on the road to recovery, it is essential to identify your red flags. The triggers, warning signs, and high-risk situations that could cause you to relapse. The truth of the matter is that we seldom get ourselves into these situations by accident. Often, we set ourselves up to get drawn in, and then it leads us into a downward spiral and we find ourselves trying to swim upstream. That is why examining the triggers that often lead to relapse or repeating past mistakes is crucial.

Triggers come in different shapes and sizes, and they are personalized for everyone. However, it is essential to recognize the various warning signs and situations that could trigger cravings, urges, and previous bad behaviors. For instance, here is a list of multiple situations and warning signs that may affect you. As you read through this list, be honest with yourself and try to determine which situations are your biggest challenges:

Social Settings

Being around friends or acquaintances who engage in the behavior you are trying to avoid.

Attending parties or events where substances or tempting behaviors are prevalent.

Feeling peer pressure to conform to certain behaviors or habits.

Emotional States

Experiencing intense stress, anxiety, or depression.

Feeling lonely or isolated.

Dealing with boredom or restlessness.

Environmental Triggers

Being in places associated with previous indulgence or addiction.

Exposure to advertisements, media, or social media content that promotes the behavior or substance you are trying to avoid.

Having access to items or objects directly related to the behavior or substance.

Emotional Triggers

Experiencing strong emotions such as anger, sadness, stress, or frustration.

Facing conflicts or relationship difficulties.

Dealing with traumatic or life-changing events.

Places, People, and Things

Revisiting the places where you previously used or have fallen.

Being around people who have negatively influenced you.

Items that remind you of your past life.

Negative Self-Talk and Mindset

Engaging in negative self-talk or self-doubt.

Having low self-esteem or feelings of unworthiness.

Believing that giving in to the cravings or urges will provide relief or escape.

This is not an exhaustive list, and triggers can vary from person to person. The key is becoming aware of your red flags and then develop strategies to cope with or avoid them. By understanding your motivations, you can better prepare yourself to navigate life's minefields and maintain your progress toward a healthier and more fulfilling life.

AN ANXIOUS WAIT

For two months, my brother Nick found himself confined to a lonely motel room, anxiously awaiting his looming court date. Sadly, being in isolation and alone was a trigger for him. Desperately trying to stay sober, he grappled with the overwhelming uncertainty of an impending court decision that seemed entirely beyond his control. He relapsed a couple of times, including the night before his trial.

When the date finally arrived, the bailiff stood ready with handcuffs, and Nick braced himself for the worst. Yet, I believe, the God of Second Chances showed up in the courtroom that day. The judge, who had been following Nick's journey through months of rehab and court appearances, offered him an unexpected lifeline—a plea deal that would drop the felonies, reducing the charges to misdemeanors. Two years of probation awaited him, along with the requirement to reside in a sober living and recovery center. It was a chance to rebuild his life, and Nick gratefully accepted.

Setting foot in a sober living house, Nick found himself among a diverse group of over a dozen men, each with their own struggles and stories. With little to his name, he was humbled by the second chance that lay before him, a path to redemption and transformation. He recognized that real change needed to take place, and with the support of the wonderful people around him, he began to find hope and his purpose.

SELF-REFLECTION AND SITUATION MAPPING

Staying on the path that God has for you is not easy. Temptations hide around every corner. Lies and deception are everywhere we turn and behind everything we click. But I am confident that with the Lord's help, reliance on others, and practice, you can get back up and keep going. There are many ways to stay on the right path, but I want to look at just a few well-researched and proven practices that have helped millions from falling again and again: self-reflection and situation mapping.

SELF-REFLECTION

Self-reflection is another aspect of identifying the triggers in your life that may cause you to slip up. However, in addition to recognizing the triggers, it is essential to try to understand the "why" behind those triggers. What is at the heart of those triggers? I realize this is a probing question, but it is crucial to ask yourself now. You cannot ask these questions when you are caught in an undertow and trying to swim against the current. You have to be prepared beforehand.

When you understand what's at the heart of the trigger, you can continuously pull back the layers to help uncover the causes and what's in your core that makes you continue to stumble. Here are just a few examples to reflect upon. Many of these will be especially helpful to those who have struggled with substance abuse or other addictive behavior, but whatever your area of temptation, you'll find these items for self-reflection useful. As you read these, ask yourself which ones resonate with you and why?

Romanticizing past experiences: You convince yourself how awesome and great your life was when you were overspending, gambling, drinking, using, etc. You make your memories bigger by exaggerating the good times and downplaying or blocking out the pain it caused you and others.

Negative thoughts about living clean: You remember the times you tried to quit in the past and don't want to go through the pain or withdrawal again. You try to convince yourself that it's awful, terrible, and unbearable to live without what you had in the past. Living a clean life sounds horrible, boring, and carries with it a list of problems of its own.

Denying your addiction: You often tell yourself you don't have an addiction problem. You say things like, "Addicts are people who can't stop, but I can stop anytime I want to."

Magical thinking: You tell yourself that a small splurge, fix, or drink can magically cure your problems or at least numb your situation. You try to convince yourself that you will only do it one more time and won't abuse it like you did last time. Then you will stop.

Failure to connect: You refuse to see the connection between your drinking, drugging, or other harmful activity and your problems. You convince yourself that you have the right to do what you want to do. It's part of your freedom, and no one has the right to make you stop.

Getting into problem situations: Perhaps there are times when you overcommit to things and need a break, or you get frustrated at work or at home, and you need to let off some steam. Maybe you're feeling lonely, a bit depressed, and believe everyone else is out there having a good time, so why can't you?

Coping mechanism: You've just faced a loss, or maybe you're feeling good about your situation, so you want to feel even better and celebrate. You use something to reward yourself or to get through a difficult time.

Associating with problem people: You want to fit in with others or at certain places, so you figure this is what it takes to be accepted. Or maybe you accidentally run into old friends who were part of your past life.

Reflecting on the people, places, and times that could cause you to slip up will help you to prepare better as you move forward. But self-reflection is only one step to managing the situation. It's also crucial to visualize what the situation may look like that causes you to stumble. Visualizing the situation in your mind will help you better prepare a future plan.

SITUATION MAPPING

The Navy SEALs are America's best of the best when it comes to completing the most dangerous missions.

During their training, the SEALs develop a multitude of contingency plans as they anticipate what might occur while they are on the battlefield attempting to accomplish a mission. These plans include possibilities for different entry points, unexpected resistance, changes in the target's behavior or location, and contingencies for the extraction of the team and the safe return to their base. The SEALs' training and expertise in special operations equip them to adapt and adjust their plans in real time based on the intelligence and situational awareness available to them. Their ability to effectively visualize and map out their responses to potentially changing circumstances is critical to their operational effectiveness and mission success.

You may not be preparing to raid the compound of a notorious terrorist, but what if I said that you are training and preparing for something even more significant? You are preparing for your survival and the future of those you love. As you move forward after messing up, you will very likely face life-and-death situations. What are you going to do? How can you prepare now for those situations so you can come out on the other end victoriously?

Just like SEALs visualize the obstacles they must overcome when completing a mission, spend a moment focusing on the factors causing you not to live your best. A situation map is meant to describe precisely what happens that causes you to slip up. It's helpful to visualize the situation in your mind as if it were a scene in a movie.

So, go ahead, and do this exercise now. Describe the exact sequences of events that occurred in your previous slipup as if you were telling a story or watching a scene from a movie. Try to remember the specific things you saw, heard, felt, or did. Be as precise as possible because having vague details will only result in vague results. Ask yourself questions like, "Who was I with?" "What were they doing?" "What was I doing?" "What else was going on around me?" "Where exactly did this happen?" "What time of day was it?" "What was I doing prior to this?" Start from the beginning and ask yourself, "What is the next thing that happened?"

As you think about what happened, and it's being mapped out

like a storyboard, consider the gaps in the action. Sometimes, the most important things we need to know to avoid relapsing in the future are hidden land mines in these action gaps. Once you can identify a gap, stop and reflect on it. Consider the situation and try remembering or imagining what happened during that gap.

This small practice of remembering and situation mapping on past mess-ups is key in moving forward. This is a small way to move forward because you can clearly identify your specific land mines. There are no common land mines. Everyone's are different. But the key for you is to clearly identify yours and think about how they affect you.

Having at least three contingency plans will help you move forward.

But simply identifying the triggers and mapping out your past relapses aren't enough. You have got to put a clear game plan together about how you will traverse these deadly land mines in the future.

As you have mapped out your past situations in your mind, now think of three intervention points where you could do something different that will keep you from falling. One plan is not good enough. It is vital that you have multiple contingency plans. What could you do differently at the situation's beginning, middle, or near the end to produce a better outcome? How could you have thought differently? How could you have managed your feelings differently? What actions needed to stop, or which ones needed to take place? Who should not have been in that situation, and who could have been there that would have been an ally and an asset?

Having at least three contingency plans will help you move forward. But this takes work. We will cover this in even more detail in the next chapter. For now, though, let's anticipate what the various roads ahead could look like for you.

THE ROAD AHEAD: RELAPSE OR REDEMPTION?

As we stand at the crossroads of your journey, let us explore one final exercise that holds the power to shape our future. Envision two contrasting scenarios: one depicting the consequences of another relapse and the other showcasing the blessings of staying on the right path. The road ahead has two destinations: relapse or redemption. The choice is up to you.

Imagine finding yourself entangled in a high-risk situation, despite your exhaustive efforts to avoid it. Circumstances beyond your control have ensnared you, leaving you momentarily frozen. Deep within, you recognize the right decision, yet you grapple with the urge to justify your circumstances. Thoughts like, *I can handle it. I've seen this before. I have been through enough training and practice to know my limits. I am stronger now and can quit or say no when I need to* surface in your mind. But unfortunately, history repeats itself. One sip or one moment of weakness morphs into an avalanche of detrimental choices, swiftly transforming your past into your present and placing your future in jeopardy once again. You are left feeling worthless, alone, and those you love are heartbroken again.

Now envision yourself in the same situation, but instead of giving in to the temptation, you can use some of the tactics you developed in your contingency plans. You take out that picture in your wallet of your family. Holding that photograph in your hand, you start to look at their faces. Instead of thinking about yourself, your thoughts turn to your future with them. You imagine future birthdays and holidays, vacations and reunions. So instead of reaching for something you know you shouldn't, you reach for your phone and call that friend, family member, or sponsor you know will support you. Or maybe you reach for your car keys and politely head for the door. You have chosen a different path. The path that the God of Second Chances wants you to take. The one that leads to healing and transformation.

As previously mentioned, in life, you will make decisions, and your decisions will make you. The decisions you make on the battlefield of temptation will determine the quality of your future life. Giving in to the enticements that surround you might feel like the easier choice, but in the bigger picture of life, they ultimately leave you empty and unsatisfied. They don't offer any real substance or lasting fulfillment. Yet, don't lose hope, because even in the midst of your struggles, there is a chance for redemption. The power to resist lies within you, strengthened by the constant love and grace of God.

In the journey of life, we encounter moments of stumbling, setbacks, and struggles that test our resolve. Just like my daughter who kept falling off her bike but eventually learned to ride, we too can find the strength to rise above our mistakes and find redemption in God's loving embrace. Throughout this chapter, we delved into key principles that can guide you toward a brighter future. We have emphasized the importance of identifying the red flags, triggers, and those subtle whispers that lure us back into the clutches of our past.

Yet, it is crucial to remember that our strength alone is limited. In times of temptation and vulnerability, we must turn to the God of Second Chances, who offers boundless strength and unwavering support. His grace is the beacon that guides us through the darkest nights and lifts us up when we stumble. As we lean on His grace, we discover that setbacks are not the end of our journey; rather, they become opportunities for God to display His infinite mercy and love.

In Christ, we find the ultimate source of grace and restoration. Through His sacrifice, He demonstrated God's unfathomable forgiveness and the lengths to which He is willing to go to mend our brokenness. It is through Him that we find redemption, as He carries our burdens and transforms our tests into public testimonies and messes into life-giving messages.

For Personal Reflection:

1. Have you identified your personal Delilah, the trigger or temptation that exerts power over you? What steps can you take to establish boundaries and protect yourself from its influence?
2. Take some time to create three contingency plans for the next time you could potentially face an unfavorable situation. What could you specifically do to avoid falling again?

For Discussion:

1. How do you view the concept of God as our heavenly Father, who loves and supports us unconditionally? How can this perspective be a source of comfort and motivation during times of struggle?
2. Share a personal experience of overcoming a trigger or high-risk situation that could have led to relapse. What strategies did you use to avoid falling into old patterns, and how did this experience strengthen your resolve?
3. Discuss the importance of self-reflection in identifying triggers and understanding the "why" behind our cravings or urges. How can this deeper understanding help us in the journey of recovery?

8

FOUR STEPS TO MOVING FORWARD

Consider it pure joy, my brothers and sisters, whenever you face trials of many kinds, because you know that the testing of your faith produces perseverance.

JAMES 1:2–3

It's been said that you are either in a trial, coming out of a trial, or about to enter a trial . . . you just don't know it yet.

Trials are part of life, and they come to each of us. They can come as an unwelcomed doctor's diagnosis, a pink slip from your boss, a terrible car accident, or even a misunderstanding with a neighbor. You have probably been through many trials and still have many more to come. The question is not if trials will come into your life, but what will your posture be when you do face trials?

THREE UNSATISFACTORY RESPONSES TO TROUBLES

In today's culture, there really are three different views of trials. One idea our world teaches is to avoid, run from, or cover up trials. If you need to break off a friendship or a relationship with a family member to avoid conflict, then do it. If you need to numb your trials by taking on more work, more debt, or more of an addiction, then just do it. Do whatever you must to avoid trials and have the easiest, most comfortable life.

Another option culture gives us today is that if you find yourself in the midst of a trial, you should whine and complain throughout the experience. Protest about your trials. Or worse, post your woes on social media and mope about them.

A third view held by some, particularly in the church world, may go so far as to say that trials are evidence that God is angry with you. Some would say that the reason you are suffering is because God is punishing you. Now there is such a thing as consequences for our actions, but this idea culminates in blaming God for trials because He is blatantly against you.

A BETTER WAY

Our world has these three approaches to trials, but what if we encountered trials so they could teach us something about ourselves and about God? As a friend of mine would often say, "Trials are our teacher, not our torture." What if whatever trial you may be facing or will face in the future isn't in your life to make you suffer, but rather, there to make you stronger and to teach you something?

As you navigate through trials, always remember that the God of Second Chances is your faithful teacher. Throughout this book, you have gained insights into His character and discovered your own identity in light of who He is. Now, as you embark on your journey of moving forward with God into a new future, I invite you to take the next four essential steps if you haven't already embraced them. These steps will further guide you on the path of growth and transformation.

STEP 1:
SURROUNDING YOURSELF WITH
A SUPPORT NETWORK

The COVID-19 pandemic did many things to shape the course of history. It disrupted the world's economy, polarized political parties, and set childhood development back several years. It also shed light on the fact that we were created and wired to live in community with others. The detrimental effects of isolation on our physical and mental well-being became glaringly apparent. Studies revealed heightened anxiety, depression, and substance misuse during 2020, highlighting the importance of human interaction.[21] God taught us through the pandemic that living in community with others and getting connected with people is vital to our physical, mental, and spiritual health. But we aren't the first ones to figure this out. In fact, there are many instances in the Scriptures where God's people traversed through their trials with help from others.

From the dawn of creation, God was aware of the inherent danger of solitude. In the narrative of Adam and Eve, we encounter the first instance where God saw something that was "not good" (Genesis 2:18). Up until this point in the creation story, everything God had made was either "good" or "very good." But what He recognized was "not good" was for humans to live in isolation without a companion. God never intended for humanity to be alone. He knew from the beginning that He would create Eve as a "helper suitable for him" (Genesis 2:18). There are several different translations of this phrase but essentially they all drive at the same point, which is that in life, we cannot and were not created to make it on our own or in isolation. We need one another.

If you thumb through the pages of Scripture, you will continue

The pages of Scripture are filled with people who believed in God but also who knew that life is too complicated to make it alone. They needed help from others. So do you.

to see helpful relationships and support networks. For instance, Moses relied heavily on his older brother, Aaron, and later his father-in-law, Jethro, who gave him some excellent advice. David required help from his faithful and loyal companion Jonathan. Jesus chose a dozen men and some women to help Him during His earthly ministry. The early church relied on and encouraged each other to proclaim the good news about the resurrection of Jesus. The pages of Scripture are filled with people who believed in God but also knew that life is too complicated to make it alone. They needed help from others. So do you.

I encourage you not to live quarantined from others and they from you. Instead, find a network of people you can trust and rely on when you need them the most. Here are a few suggestions of where you can go as you establish a support network:

Professional counseling: Research literature clearly shows that the more time you invest in professional counseling and therapy during the first two years of recovery, the more likely you will not relapse.[22] Professional groups, either individual therapy sessions, recovery educational sessions, or group therapy sessions, have proven to be highly successful for people wanting to make significant changes in their life.

Self-help programs: There are several self-help programs for various needs. For instance, groups such as Financial Peace University and Crown Financial Ministries help people get out of debt and find financial freedom. DivorceCare is a national divorce recovery network that offers support groups to those either in the middle of a divorce or after having a divorce. Alcoholics Anonymous (AA), Narcotics Anonymous (NA), Rational Recovery, and Women for Sobriety, among others, aid in helping people overcome alcohol and narcotic addictions. These groups have many things in common, including but not limited to, asking you to abstain from using, regularly attending meetings to build relationships with others, connecting you with an established member (often referred to as a sponsor), and they promote a program of designated steps to help you get back on your feet.

Church or Christian-based group: Most people recovering find the need to invest regular time in developing themselves spiritually in groups like Celebrate Recovery or through a specific recovery group their church hosts. GriefShare welcomes anyone as they process grief and loss. Whether it is a church group or a non-church Christian recovery group, at the heart of any spiritual program are three activities: (1) fellowship with others, (2) prayer and meditation with God, (3) group worship and acknowledgment that true power and redemption comes from the God of Second Chances.

These are just a few of the support networks available to you as you take your first steps toward your second chance. Remember, you are not alone. There are countless numbers of people who are there to help you. All you have to do is take the initiative to take that first step. Keep pressing forward, knowing that a vibrant community awaits you on the path to healing and transformation.

STEP 2:
SETTING GOALS AND CRAFTING
YOUR PERSONAL DEVELOPMENT PLAN

It would be a vast understatement to say that our kids are excited to discover what is inside their colorful packages at Christmastime. It is almost as if they think new toys will launch them into some thrilling adventure, and their new clothes will give them a brand-new identity. Of course, as parents, we know that their initial delight at these possessions will eventually fade.

Yet, there exists a gift of unparalleled significance, one that will never wear out or lose its luster—the free gift of salvation through Jesus Christ. When we believe in Jesus as our Savior, we begin a new journey with a new purpose. We no longer identify with the ways of the world, but our identity can be found in Christ, who will take us on a journey we never expected. He gives us a new way to live.

The apostle Paul writes that "if anyone is in Christ, the new creation has come" (2 Corinthians 5:17). Once a person accepts Christ's offer of salvation, he or she has been reborn, or re-created. Notice that Paul uses the word "anyone." The city of Corinth was a significant trading post with people coming and going from various nations and cultures. However, Paul wants his readers to know that regardless of where each individual came from, anyone and everyone is welcome to be "in Christ" (v. 17). When we are "in Christ," we are transformed into a new creation. Paul wants his readers to know that followers of Jesus are not just forgiven of their sins but made into someone completely new. Did you know that the moment you put your trust in Christ, you became a new person with a new purpose and future?

You might be wondering, "What is my new purpose?" According

to Paul, we are called to be ambassadors of Christ, representing Him through our lives (v. 20). However, being a new creation and His ambassador doesn't mean we will be perfect. It means that we undergo an ongoing process of transformation. The power of God works within us to continually shape and refine our character.

> *"Practice makes permanent." Permanent behaviors are what you are striving for.*

So, as you take the first steps on your new journey moving forward with Him, it is essential to set goals and craft a plan on how you want to develop your new life. Recovery is a learned set of behaviors, and like any behavior or habit, to keep it, we must practice it. Some say, "Practice makes perfect." But your goal is not to be perfect. Only Jesus is perfect. Instead, it is better to say, "Practice makes permanent." Permanent behaviors are what you are striving for. A perpetual lifestyle that glorifies God and enjoys life His way.

Start by identifying specific goals in different areas of your life: personal, professional, relational, and spiritual. For instance, your personal goals could be centered around having a proper diet and exercise plan. Having goals in these areas has proven to immensely help those on the road to recovery. What you eat and how much or little exercise you partake in directly correlate to your thinking, feeling, and acting. A healthy diet and exercise schedule will help you feel less anxious and depressed and better about yourself.[23]

You may need to set up professional goals like implementing better time-management skills. Perhaps you would like to obtain a certificate or degree to help enhance your professional skills to advance your career. Whatever it may be, take steps to improve your personal life so that your habits become permanent.

Relational goals are a bit more challenging because they often involve somebody else. But try to build your relationship goals around things that you can control. For instance, maybe set a goal of wanting to talk to ten strangers every week. Or maybe write letters or send texts to all your family members at least once a month. Set relational goals that help you to reach out and improve your inter-personal skills.

Spiritual goals are vital because often the closer we are to God, and the stronger our relationship is with Him, the more likely our thoughts and actions begin to align with His will for our lives. There-fore, setting daily goals such as Bible reading and prayer is important. But in addition to these, get plugged into a church or volunteer for a ministry. Grow your spiritual life daily, and as you learn and serve, you will see your life through God's lens.

Writing down your goals and the steps you'll take to reach them will give you guideposts to follow, milestones to accomplish. As much as possible, make your goals measurable and achievable. Aim for something you can fulfill soon. For example, instead of deter-mining to read your Bible for an hour each day for a year, make it your goal to read a chapter daily for a week. Then do it again the next week. Breaking down your goals in each of these areas into doable bites will not only improve your life but will give you a satisfying sense of achievement and the confidence to continue. You might also appropriately share some of your goals with another person.

Think about how you can break down these goals into smaller, achievable steps. What phone calls do you need to make today? What books do you need to buy now? What class do you need to sign up for this week? Create a timeline of when you will accomplish these things and get someone to hold you accountable. Starting something new can be intimidating. But with help from others and Christ as your guide, your new journey will be worth it.

STEP 3:
SEEKING AMENDS AND
RESTORING CONNECTIONS

We have discussed this in previous chapters, but it is such a critical component to moving forward that it is necessary to discuss it again here. Just as we can't move forward without some sort of support group, we can't move forward without trying to mend and restore relationships with those we have hurt in the past.

This may be the most difficult of all the steps because it involves family, friends, coworkers, and people we know who are close to us. The enemy of your soul, Satan, wants nothing but conflict, pain, and suffering to continue. However, the gospel teaches us a different story. If God has forgiven us for all the sins in our lives, we ought to be able to forgive others who have sinned against us. Likewise, if we can ask God to forgive us, we should humble ourselves and ask for forgiveness from those we have hurt.

It must have stunk, literally and figuratively, for the prodigal son in Jesus' parable in Luke 15:11–32. It is one of Jesus' most famous stories. I mentioned it before, but it is worth mentioning again. It begins with a young man who squanders his father's inheritance. He reaches the point where he was hired to feed pigs on someone else's farm. Talk about a smelly job. Except he wasn't bringing home the bacon, again, literally and figuratively. Jesus says that he was so hungry that he "longed to fill his stomach with the pods that the pigs were eating, but no one gave him anything" (v. 16). Realizing his situation and acknowledging his life was on a downward trajectory, he came to his senses, and sought forgiveness from his father.

None of us relishes the thought of approaching those we have hurt the most and asking for forgiveness. Yet, in order to live the life God desires for us, restoring these relationships is essential. Take intentional steps to reach out, whether through a heartfelt letter, a phone call, or a face-to-face conversation. Ask for their forgiveness and express genuine remorse. Keep in mind that their response is beyond your control; forgiveness is a personal journey for each individual. They may not be ready to extend forgiveness, and that is okay. What matters is that you extend a hand of forgiveness and take responsibility for your part in the relationship. By doing so, you create space for healing and growth, enabling you to move forward.

One more thing about that story Jesus told about the son who squandered his father's inheritance. It is perhaps one of the most well-known stories from Jesus. But it is actually the third and final story in a string of parables that Jesus used for a specific purpose. He was critiquing the religious leaders. The Pharisees were again critical that Jesus was associating with sinners and tax collectors. Each parable Jesus told highlighted the rejoicing after something lost is eventually found.

We can easily relate to each story because there is a person who is devasted by what was lost, but then rejoicing ensues once it is found. For instance, the shepherd leaves the ninety-nine and looks for the lost sheep (Luke 15:4–7). The woman lights a lamp, using precious oil, to look for her lost coin (Luke 15:8–10). However, have you ever noticed that in the third parable, no one goes to look for the lost son? In the first-century culture, it was often the responsibility of the oldest son to go and look for his younger brother. That's right, in Jesus' parable of the prodigal son, there are actually two sons. One that represents those in need of a second chance, and the elder son who represents the most religious people of the day. Yet, in Jesus' parable, the elder son stays home and leaves his father to anxiously wait for the younger son to return (v. 20).

When the younger son eventually returned, the father was elated and celebrated with the entire community (v. 22–24). However, the older son was aghast and angered. How could the father forgive his brother, who humiliated the family name, squandered the wealth, and lived a sinful lifestyle (vv. 25–30)?

When the Pharisees heard this parable and realized Jesus was comparing them to the older son, they too must have been astonished that Jesus would welcome sinners into the kingdom. As the religious experts, it was their duty to go after those that were lost, but they were too self-righteous to give others a second chance. But God is constantly seeking the lost and so should all who believe that God gives second chances.

In this short parable, I easily thought of my brother as the prodigal son. For me, it was easy to see the similarities. He left our hometown under a cloud of conflict. We hardly heard from him. We knew he was getting into things he shouldn't have, and we were waiting for the day he would eventually hit rock bottom, realize he was lost, and come to his senses.

What I constantly failed to realize, though, was that I was acting like the other brother. Instead of going out to look for him and helping to bring him home, I pretended like it was someone else's problem. I secretly thought, *If he got himself into this mess, he could get himself out.* However, I failed to realize that it was my duty, as a believer in the God of Second Chances, to go and look for him and bring him back to a healthy relationship with the family.

Thankfully, the God of Second Chances continues to work in my life, and unlike the older son or the Pharisees, I get to enjoy being the director of the "Welcome Home" party. If you have experienced God's forgiveness, make it your mission to seek others who need another chance too. Then join the celebration!

Remember, the road to restoration is not easy for anyone, but it is necessary. Trust in God's grace to guide you as you seek to repair the broken bonds. Allow humility and sincerity to be your companions along this journey of reconciliation. In taking these courageous steps, you open the door to healing and transformation, both for yourself and for those whose lives you have touched.

STEP 4:
EMPOWERING OTHERS THROUGH
YOUR JOURNEY

Imagine you were invited to the table, that table. The table where Jesus shared a meal with His friends before the Passover Feast. As you eagerly await the festivities, something unexpected unfolds. Jesus rises, takes a towel and a basin of water, and begins to wash everyone's feet. This was supposed to be the job of the servant of the house, not the master of the house. At the very least, it was your job. He shouldn't be washing your feet—you should be washing His! But Jesus teaches His disciples, as well as you and me, that being His follower means getting into the foot washing business. Christ gives us a new way to live by showing us a new way to love.

One of the exciting things about what Jesus did at that table was actually the timing of His act of service. Jesus knew that the time for His departure and death was just hours away. He knew the pain, torture, mockery, and betrayal that would soon be inflicted upon Him. Nevertheless, He used the opportunity around the table with friends to teach them how to love one another. It is impossible to say what you or I would do if we were at that table many years ago, but today we are called to live out a similar love as Jesus showed His friends.

God has brought you on an incredible journey, and He is far from finished with you. There are feet to be washed and a story to be shared. He longs to transform your mess into a message that can shape the lives of others. So, seize every opportunity to serve others by vulnerably sharing your triumphs and trials. Through your own experiences, you have gained invaluable insights about yourself, about God, and about resilience. Now it is time for others to benefit from those lessons through you.

You didn't know this at the time, but it is very possible that the reason you went through the things you did was so that you could help someone else. Your story is important, and if the God of Second Chances is at the center of it, its power surpasses your wildest imagination. I can guarantee that the enemy wants your story to remain silent. Think about it, from the time of Jesus to today, the enemy has wanted believers in Jesus to keep quiet. Fear, shame, embarrassment, and even persecution have been employed to prevent people from sharing the extraordinary work the God of Second Chances had done in their lives. However, a bold message necessitates bold messengers.

Peter and John, dear friends of Jesus, understood this truth. Despite being arrested and forbidden to speak about Jesus, they continued to boldly share their story shortly after encountering the risen Christ. Luke, the writer of the book of Acts, records their response to the authorities who demanded they stay silent, "Which is right in God's eyes: to listen to you, or to him? . . . We cannot help speaking about what we have seen and heard" (Acts 4:19–20). Nor should you.

Don't stop sharing your journey and your story. God is in the business of turning your tests into a testimony. Your past has the potential to change someone's future. Who is seated at your "table" whom you are called to love? How can you serve them today, and with whom can you share your remarkable story, even if it is still unfolding? Embrace your role as an agent of change, knowing that your influence can bring hope, healing, and transformation to someone who desperately needs it. Trust in God's unwavering faithfulness as you continue to impact lives through your journey of redemption.

Less than a year after my brother faced that life-altering decision in front of a judge, he found himself standing at a crossroads once again. This time, however, it wasn't about him; it was about how he could use his own journey of redemption to help others struggling to move forward after messing up.

Within a few months of settling in at his recovery house, something remarkable happened—Nick's dedication and commitment to change caught the attention of the house leaders. Their trust in him grew, and they rewarded his hard work by appointing him as a house manager, a role of responsibility and mentorship over his fellow residents. As a house manager, Nick's purpose extended beyond his own recovery. It was now to guide and mentor his fellow residents, walking side by side with them on their paths to healing. The turnaround was astonishing, a testament to the power of second chances and the strength that comes from a supportive community.

But the story didn't end there. The sober living organization recognized Nick's passion for helping others and offered him yet another chance to make a difference—to become a peer-recovery coach. A few months later, he embraced the opportunity where he could pour out his heart and soul, using his own journey as a guiding light for others who needed to find their way forward.

Today, Nick's mission is clear, and his purpose is unwavering. He has been able to move out of the house, get his own apartment, and meets and coaches others by sharing his story of hope and resilience to inspire them to rewrite their own narratives. As if that weren't enough, he also leads group teaching sessions, imparting the wisdom and tools the participants need to overcome addiction and reclaim their lives. He has sought out additional classes, invested countless hours in volunteering, and sought supervision to achieve his new goal of becoming a certified peer and family specialist. Through him, countless souls will discover the courage to rise again and embrace the second chance that the God of Second Chances graciously offers.

FINDING THE COURAGE TO STEP FORWARD AND EMBRACE THE HEALING TOUCH

When someone is skilled at caring for the needs of the sick, we might say they have a "healing touch." However, no one has ever shown the extraordinary power to heal like Jesus. In Mark's account of the life of Jesus, he records Jesus' healing touch over many areas of life. First, in Mark 4:35–41, Jesus demonstrated His power over nature when He calmed the "furious squall" that arose on the water (v. 37). Then, in Mark 5:1–20, Jesus restored a demon-possessed man to health, displaying His power over the darkness. In Mark 5:21–43, the healing climaxes when Jesus exhibits His authority over sickness and death.

There are actually two stories within Mark 5:21–43 that are meant to be compared and contrasted. In scene one, a synagogue leader, Jairus, approaches Jesus and pleads with Him for help because his daughter is on the verge of dying. In scene two, on their way to Jairus' home, a woman who had been suffering from severe bleeding for twelve long years secretly approaches Jesus from behind and gently touches His cloak.

According to the custom, this woman would have been considered unclean because of her bleeding. She was a social outcast, unable to worship at the temple courts (vv. 25–26). Jairus' daughter, by contrast, grew up happy and healthy, seeing her father come and go regularly to the synagogue as one of the leaders (v. 22). Even though they came from different social standings, both Jairus and the woman showed a similar faith in Jesus. They both believed He had the healing touch. They also both had a decision to make. "To get the help I truly need, I have to muster up the courage and reach out to Jesus."

It took courage for both individuals to reach out to Jesus for help. No doubt, a bit of timidity was running through their veins. However, they realized that nothing and no one else could help them in their desperate time of need. Through their courageous act of reaching out, their faith in Jesus led to healing—for themselves and their family members (vv. 34, 36). Mark makes it clear that these narratives prove that God Himself is the only one who has authority over nature, the powers of darkness, sickness, and even death to truly heal. The same is true for you and whatever you are facing.

For Personal Reflection

1. Reflect on a trial you've recently faced or are currently experiencing. What lessons do you think this trial is teaching you about yourself and your relationship with God?
2. How can you apply the concept of "practice makes permanent" to your personal development plan and recovery journey?

For Discussion:

1. Discuss the significance of building a support network during the recovery process. How can the group encourage and support one another in times of trial?

2. Share personal goals you have set for yourself during your recovery journey. How do you plan to achieve these goals, and how can the group support you in your efforts?

3. Talk about how you can use your own journey of recovery to empower others. How can you share your story in a way that brings hope and healing to those who may be struggling?

➤ ➤ ➤ ➤ ➤

I am so proud of you for reading this book. If you have started to put into motion some steps to get you back on your feet, I'm thrilled. But if you genuinely want to be healed, forgiven, freed, loved, restored, cherished, known, and whole, find the courage to reach out to Jesus. If you have messed up, He is the only way to truly move forward. I hope you can and do because only the God of Second Chances has the "healing touch."

ACKNOWLEDGMENTS

Moving forward with anything is a journey that takes a team. This book is no exception.

The first group of people I want to thank are those who have helped me traverse the paths of writing and publication. I have many past professors and mentors I could thank, but two have helped me the most on this journey. Dr. Scott Gibson, thanks for always inspiring me to be a writer and learner. Dr. John Koessler, thank you for taking me under your wing at the Moody Bible Institute both as a student and then as a colleague. I especially appreciate you encouraging me to write for Moody's monthly devotional *Today in the Word*, and introducing me to Jamie Janosz, the general editor. Jamie, thanks for taking a chance on me as a young writer and giving me an opportunity to test my writing skills. Your direction for the June 2022 issue of "God of Second Chances" was the impetus for this book. Thank you for connecting me to Drew Dyck, my acquisitions editor at Moody Publishers. Drew, your support, guidance, and collaboration have been extremely life-giving. The team at Moody Publishers have been top-notch and first-class from start to finish. I especially enjoyed working with Pam Pugh, my developmental editor. Pam, your ability to make me sound much better than I am is an incredible skill and second only to your wit and humor.

Next, I want to thank those who have walked this journey with me the longest. This book is personal because I am able to share stories about family and friends who have shared their inspiring stories with me. To Peter Dahlin, your guidance and unwavering support on the path of the Lord have been invaluable. Thanks to my mother, Janet Rappazini, and sister, Jenny Parker—your presence as sounding boards and shoulders to lean on has been a source of great strength. Thanks to Ken Gay for marrying my mother after my father passed away, and also for the wisdom you shared with me, and the passion you have for leading recovery groups and helping people get back on their feet.

The next group of people I want to express my gratitude to are the ones who call me husband and dad. Ashley, I'm thankful for your unwavering support, for allowing me the time to slip away to write, and for always being my first reader. To my three little kids, Adeline, Thomas, and Graham, thanks for all the unexpected interruptions you gave me during this process that came when I needed them the most. As you grow older, remember that no matter what life presents, both your mother and I and the God of Second Chances are here for you.

Last but not least, I want to extend my heartfelt appreciation to my brother, Nick Rappazini, for graciously allowing me to share aspects of your journey. Your strength and resilience serve as a boundless source of inspiration, not only for me but for countless others as well. Your generosity is matchless, and your ability to overcome challenges is truly remarkable.

NOTES

1. "Modane Train Crash of 1917," *Encyclopedia Britannica*, December 5, 2022, https://www.britannica.com/event/Modane-train-crash-of-1917.

2. Christopher Rappazini, *Today in the Word*, June 22, 2022, https://www.todayintheword.org/issues/2022/god-of-second-chances/daily-devotional/you-are-forgiven/. Used with permission.

3. Joseph Stowell, *Why It's Hard to Love Jesus* (Chicago: Moody Publishers, 2003).

4. A. W. Tozer, *The Knowledge of the Holy* (New York: HarperOne, 1961), 1.

5. Ibid., 39.

6. S.L. Price, "SI Vault: The Gospel according to Ray," *Sports Illustrated*, July 7, 2015, https://www.si.com/nfl/2015/07/07/ray-lewis-baltimore-ravens-sports-illustrated-2006-cover-story.

7. To read Joseph's full story, turn to Genesis 37; 39–45.

8. If you are interested in learning more about the animosity between Jews and Samaritans, see "What Is a Samaritan?," https://www.gotquestions.org/what-is-a-Samaritan.html.

9. Rick Warren, *The Purpose Driven Life, Expanded Edition* (Grand Rapids, MI: Zondervan, 2012), 149.

10. This quote is widely attributed to Thomas of Villanova, 1486–1555. Thomas was known for his charitable works and for his writings.

11. Matthew T. Lee et al., "From Defiance to Reliance: Spiritual Virtue as a Pathway Towards Desistence, Humility, and Recovery among Juvenile Offenders," *Spirituality in Clinical Practice* 4, no. 3 (2017): 161–75. Also see Stephen G. Post et al., "Humility and 12-Step Recovery: A Prolegomenon for the Empirical Investigation of a Cardinal Virtue in Alcoholics Anonymous," *Alcoholism Treatment Quarterly* 34, no. 3 (2016): 262–73.

12. Frank Wang, Keith J. Edwards, and Peter C. Hill, "Humility as a Relational Virtue: Establishing Trust, Empowering Repair, and Building Marital Well-Being," *Journal of Psychology and Christianity* 36, no. 2 (2017): 168.

13. For further research, read Tenelle Porter and Karina Schumann, "Intellectual Humility and Openness to the Opposing View," *Self and Identity* 17, no. 2 (2018): 139–62. Also read J. Andrew, Morris, Céleste M. Brotheridge, and John C. Urbanski, "Bringing Humility to Leadership: Antecedents and Consequences of Leader Humility," *Human Relations* 58, no. 10 (2005): 1323–50.

14. Carol S. Dweck, *Mindset: The New Psychology of Success* (New York: Ballantine, 2016).

15. Rachel Treisman, "A Lobster Diver in Cape Cod Says a Humpback Whale Scooped Him Up and Spat Him Out," NPR, June 11, 2021, https://www.npr.org/2021/06/12/1005918788/humpback-whale-swallowed-lobster-diver-cape-cod-michael-packard.

16. John Bunyan, *The Pilgrim's Progress*.

17. Joss Whedon, director, *The Avengers*, Marvel Studios, 2012.

18. "For if, while we were God's enemies, we were reconciled to him through the death of his Son, how much more, having been reconciled, shall we be saved through his life!" (Romans 5:10); "If you confess with your mouth that Jesus is Lord and believe in your heart that God raised him from the dead, you will be saved" (Romans 10:9 ESV); "For what I received I passed on to you as of first importance: that Christ died for our sins according to the Scriptures, that he was buried, that he was raised on the third day according to the Scriptures" (1 Corinthians 15:3–4); "Praise be to the God and Father of our Lord Jesus Christ! In his great mercy he has given us new birth into a living hope through the resurrection of Jesus Christ from the dead" (1 Peter 1:3).

19. *Merriam-Webster.com Dictionary*, s.v. "resilient (adj.)," https://www.merriam-webster.com/dictionary/resilient.

20. Max Lucado, *A Gentle Thunder: Hearing God Through the Storm* (Nashville, TN: Thomas Nelson, 2012), 115.

21. Tonya Cross Hansel et al., "COVID-19 Behavioral Health and Quality of Life," *Scientific Reports* 12, no. 1 (2022): 961; Emanuele Caroppo et al., "Will Nothing Be the Same Again?: Changes in Lifestyle During COVID-19 Pandemic and Consequences on Mental Health," *International Journal of Environmental Research and Public Health* 18, no. 16 (2021): 8433; Peter A. Hall et al., "Biobehavioral Aspects of the COVID-19 Pandemic: A Review," *Psychosomatic Medicine* 83, no. 4 (2021): 309.

22. David Capuzzi and Mark D. Stauffer, *Counseling and Psychotherapy: Theories and Interventions* (Hoboken, NJ: John Wiley & Sons, 2016); Douglas L. Polcin, "Professional Counseling Versus Specialized Programs for Alcohol and Drug Abuse Treatment," *Journal of Addictions & Offender Counseling* 21, no. 1 (2000): 2–11.

23. Jennifer Cowan and Carol Devine, "Food, Eating, and Weight Concerns of Men in Recovery from Substance Addiction," *Appetite* 50, no. 1 (2008): 33–42.

Is joy the icing on the cake of life—
or the fuel on which it runs?

ONE THING KEEPS US
FROM A COMPELLING LIFE:
WE ARE STUCK.

Organized around the most significant event of the prophet Elijah's life, his cave experience, *Unstuck* helps you discover what is holding you back from starting a new chapter of life. Mark Jobe will help you address your unfinished business, rediscover your boundaries, break out of isolation, and re-envision your life story to step out of your cave and into your call.

Also available as eBook